# A HANDBOOK FOR COUNSELING THE GIFTED AND TALENTED

## Barbara Kerr, PhD

With contribution. ..к Hallowell, PhD
and Stephen Schroeder-Davis

Foreword by Nicholas Colangelo, PhD

**AMERICAN COUNSELING ASSOCIATION**

5999 Stevenson Avenue
Alexandria, VA 22304-3300

(AACD became the American Counseling Association on July 1, 1992)

American Counseling Association
5999 Stevenson Avenue
Alexandria, VA 22304

Cover design by Sarah Jane Valdez

**Library of Congress Cataloging-in-Publication Data**

Kerr, Barbara.
    Handbook for counseling gifted and talented / Barbara Kerr ; with
contributions by Kirk Hallowell and Stephen Schroeder-Davis ; foreword by
Nicholas Colangelo.
        p.    cm.
    Includes bibliographical references.
    ISBN 1-55620-079-X
    1. Gifted children—Education—United States.   2. Gifted children—
Counseling of—United States.   3. Personnel service in education—United
States.   I. Hallowell, Kirk.   II. Title.
LC3993.9.K47      1990
371.95'0973—dc20                                                    90-45712
                                                                    CIP

Printed in the United States of America
(Third Printing)

*To my husband and colleague, Chuck Claiborn*

# Contents

# *Resources*

# Foreword

Gifted education has received considerable attention the last several years compared to previous years. One of the most exciting current features, in my estimation, is the recognition of counseling needs. Although the initial concern for the social and emotional needs of the gifted can be traced back to the pioneering work of Leta Hollingworth, these aspects have never had a major or consistent focus in gifted education.

*A Handbook for Counseling the Gifted and Talented* is a welcome addition to the fields of counseling and gifted education. As a counselor educator, I am aware that school counselors rarely receive any formal preparation for conceptualizing and meeting the counseling needs of gifted students. Most counselors rely on common sense and general counseling skills when dealing with gifted youngsters. It has been my experience that more and more school counselors are "discovering" that gifted students have unique needs, and these counselors are seeking assistance in responding to these needs. This handbook is written for such counselors.

Barbara Kerr writes in a straightforward yet personal style. She writes with the confidence of someone who has spent many years counseling with gifted students and administering counseling-focused programs. Her introductory comments on Mike Darwood, an unrecognized genius, set a personal tone for the book.

Kerr states that the handbook is organized as a "practical guide to the counselor who is working with gifted students." The book contains practical suggestions in a number of counselor areas. I was especially pleased to see chapters on academic guidance (chapter 2) and career counseling (chapter 5). Both these chapters bring the subject of counseling gifted students well into the mainstream of school counseling.

Kerr's reputation for her clinical and research work regarding gifted girls makes chapter 6, "Counseling Gifted and Talented Girls," a very strong part of the book. She has translated for counselors the important issues that concern gifted girls and gifted women. I found this chapter most informative.

I believe *A Handbook for Counseling the Gifted and Talented* will prove a very useful resource for counselors. Teachers and parents would also benefit from this book. As school counselors recognize that gifted students do have specialized counseling needs, the *Handbook* will serve them very well in their professional work.

*—Nicholas Colangelo*
*Myron & Jacqueline Blank Professor of Gifted Education and*
*Director of The Connie Belin National Center for Gifted Education*

# *Acknowledgments*

Many people contributed their knowledge and skills to the preparation of this book. Kirk Hallowell and Stephen Schroeder-Davis both contributed major efforts. Kirk Hallowell's theory of academic guidance of gifted students was developed over the course of many years' experience administering and teaching summer institutes for gifted students at Drury College's Summerscape, the Missouri Scholars' Academy, and the Iowa Governor's Institute. Stephen Schroeder-Davis very kindly lent the results of his dissertation study on books for gifted students to this book. His splendid annotated bibliography is in the Resources section of this book.

Paula Brandt of the Curriculum Laboratory of The University of Iowa College of Education prepared several booklists oriented toward gifted girls' concerns and careers for gifted students. Cathann Arcenaux developed the underachievers intervention described in the Resources section of this book, as well as enlightening me about many characteristics and needs of the underachieving gifted. Sandra Berger's idea about college planning for gifted students was an important influence; I recommend her book, *College Planning for Gifted Students*, as a companion to this one.

My graduate assistant, Li Fang Zhang, was a tireless researcher, locating hard-to-find sources and working overtime to proofread chapters. Pam Bullers organized me and my materials and kept me on task throughout the process of preparation. Reta Litton and Ginny Travis typed the manuscript many times and were always far ahead of my deadlines. My current graduate assistant, Susan Maresh, helped put the finishing touches on the manuscript.

My mentor and colleague, Nick Colangelo, provided the excellent resources of the Connie Belin National Center for Gifted Education and has been my closest collaborator on the many studies of the gifted and talented described throughout this book.

Finally, thanks to all the student counselors at the Guidance Laboratory for Gifted and Talented at the University of Nebraska and the Counseling Laboratory for Talent Development at The University of Iowa, who taught me even as they learned about counseling gifted students.

# Author and
# Contributor
# Notes

Barbara Kerr is now professor of psychology in education at Arizona State University in Tempe, Arizona. During the writing of this handbook, she was associate professor of counselor education and associate director of the Connie Belin National Center for Gifted Education.

Kirk Hallowell is visiting assistant professor, teaching in the area of student development, at Western Illinois University in Macomb, Illinois.

Stephen Schroeder-Davis is adjunct professor of gifted education and a doctoral candidate at the University of St. Thomas and St. Mary's College in St. Paul, Minnesota.

# *Prologue*

During my graduate training at Ohio State University, I had a unique opportunity to serve as the student personnel assistant for students in the Honors Program. One group of honors students was special indeed; they were the 13- to 16-year-old boys and girls enrolled as math and science majors. These prodigies were part of the university's effort to attract and train the most promising intellects. My task was to ensure that these bright young people had the supervision, guidance, and friendship that they and all adolescents need, despite their extraordinary intellectual advancement. The boy who helped me to learn the most about the needs of gifted and talented young people was Mike Darwood.

Mike was 14 years old when I met him. He was taking a variety of undergraduate and graduate level courses, and was being simultaneously courted by the math, physics, and astronomy departments. Mike was virtually a self-taught genius. He had been fascinated by math as long as he could remember. He'd had a few good teachers, but by the time he was 11, they couldn't keep up with him. Most of his teachers seemed unaware of his special gifts. His parents were unsupportive, believing his obsession with mathematics was somehow abnormal. His only resources were the books in the public library of his small town; this led to some odd knowledge gaps. For example, he read everything he could find on relativity theory, and then went on to explore the Unified Theory, on which Einstein had been working at the time of his death. Mike realized Einstein was using a form of mathematics with which he was unfamiliar: Mike had never seen calculus. So he deduced, or recreated, calculus for himself, with his own idiosyncratic symbols. At 13, Mike's excitement about his work had reached a feverish pitch because he believed he had discovered a small but interesting flaw in one part of Einstein's work.

He wrote all his ideas out; they came to two pages of equations. Knowing no other outlet, he submitted his two pages as his science fair project.

Mike's entry in the school science fair was met with universal derision. "You call this a science fair project?" said one teacher. "Two pieces of paper with math problems? A science fair project is *built* on a platform. It demonstrates something, with good use of audiovisual materials."

Mike's next entry in the county fair, under an assumed name, had better fortune. "Ikem Doowrad's" science fair project was indeed *built*, on a gaily painted plywood platform, as large as the rules allowed. There were blinking lights and a siren-like noisebox hooked into a light-sensitive device, which set off the entire display whenever anyone walked by. Above the siren, among the blinking lights, were tacked two pages of equations, Mike's comments on the Unified Theory. As luck would have it, one of the judges was familiar with advanced math and physics. The siren and blinking lights performed their function and drew this judge's attention. The judge quickly relayed the equations to a colleague in physics, who said something to the effect that "The Einsteinian notation is obsolete, there are some strange symbols that appear to be a personal form of calculus, but he's definitely got something here. Give him the prize." This was how Ikem Doowrad, or Mike Darwood, went on to the state, national, and eventually the international science fair, and this was how this obscure, self-taught genius of 13 came to the attention of the university faculty.

What I learned from Mike's story was the sad truth that great talent is often hidden, and sometimes our most brilliant students need sirens and blinking lights to get our attention. This handbook is an attempt to bring the needs of gifted students to counselors' attention so that the sirens and blinking lights will not be needed.

# Introduction

Often a counselor's first introduction to the needs and concerns of gifted students is a bright student whose behaviors are so different from the norm that he or she comes to the attention of the guidance office. Cases that attract counselors' interest to issues of giftedness might include a high-achieving student who unexpectedly gets in trouble with the law; a high-IQ student who seems to be deliberately failing classes; or a student with broad interests and talents in a wide variety of areas who seems paralyzed by the need to make a career decision. These cases are jolting because they are at odds with the stereotype of gifted students prevalent in society at large as well as in education circles: that gifted students "have it all together." The stereotype is partly the result of a tendency to generalize the concept of giftedness to all behaviors that are socially desirable.

In the case of educators, the stereotype usually arises from a brief exposure in an education class to the best-known study of gifted students—that of Lewis Terman, which began in 1921. Terman's group of high-IQ children were a sample of mainly White, middle-class,

California elementary students who had been selected by their teachers for testing (Terman, 1925). Most in this group were found to be achieving across school subjects, physically and mentally healthy, and extremely well-adjusted socially. That this sample was probably not representative of high-IQ students in general; that children of rare and specific talents were not included; and that the findings of psychological adjustment did not hold true for children at the highest IQ levels are facts generally not reported in textbooks or college classrooms. Most of us are content to operate according to a stereotype based on minimal or flawed information until we meet the child who shakes us out of our complacency.

The counselor who has decided to learn about the needs of gifted students and to provide differentiated services may face an uphill battle from teachers, administrators, and his or her own colleagues. Teachers are often unsupportive of differentiated counseling for gifted students because of negative experiences they have had with differentiated education.

Many teachers are aware that some gifted programs use ambiguous or capricious identification procedures. They may have seen pull-out programs of 2 or 3 hours a week of enrichment activities that lack planning or substance. Regular classroom teachers may resent the disruption of their usual activities for a program they find questionable. In addition, teachers may feel that gifted education programs are elitist and entail special privileges, particularly when the children selected are mostly upper-middle-class, advantaged White children. Other teachers feel pressured to provide special education for gifted students in the classroom, where there also may be students with a variety of disabilities, behavior disorders, and other special conditions requiring individualized attention. For these teachers, services for the gifted represent one more aspect of trying to be everything to everybody.

Administrators, too, have felt pressures that have made them wary of programs for gifted students. State guidelines and formulae for funding gifted education often involve rigid definitions and cutoffs that don't work well for all districts. Administrators must often find volunteer teachers, retrain teachers, or try to hire gifted educators from a scarce market.

Finally, although the vast majority of parents of bright students are supportive of and cooperative with the schools, every administrator can think of one parent who has made life miserable for the administrator, the teacher, and his or her own children with angry demands and unreasonable expectations. One such parent can sour an entire school district on the idea of gifted education.

A counselor's own colleagues may be skeptical about the counselor's interest in gifted students. "What's good for gifted students is good for all students" they may say, or "I'm too busy helping those who are almost certain to fail to be able to help those who are almost certain to succeed." The counselor determined to develop his or her skills in counseling gifted students thus may find the process thankless and solitary.

On the other hand, counseling gifted students has extraordinary rewards. The gifted are among the most challenging clients the counselor will ever see. Gifted students often have fine critical skills; they are able to analyze the counseling process and often give the counselor feedback on the effectiveness of his or her strategies. Although this can be disconcerting, it is also a way of learning about one's own skills. Gifted students are curious about the counseling process. They want to learn what the counselor knows, believes, and values. They are insightful and often demonstrate a complex and articulate understanding of themselves. Counselors can receive as much intellectual challenge from counseling gifted clients as teachers invariably say they receive from teaching advanced and honors courses with the brightest students.

Gifted students, because of their great capacity for learning, are able to manifest new ideas as new behaviors. This capacity for learning new behaviors means that both counselor and client are able to see the results of their work together.

Finally, gifted clients appreciate the help they receive. Many gifted students who have visited our counseling laboratory for talent development have told us it was the first time they felt they had been taken seriously by adults. Bright students seem to understand what they have been given by the counselor who has taken the time to listen, to gather and share information, and, together with the client, to work toward the client's goals. Their gratitude extends long past the time of their final counseling session. They write long and lively letters; they send poetry; they decorate the counselor's office with their cartoons and artwork. They write to tell articulately and passionately of the events of their lives and the events in the worlds of science, the arts, politics, business, and education.

## A History of Guiding the Gifted

Roberta Myers and Terry Pace (1986) provided a comprehensive history of counselors' concerns for gifted and talented students. According to these authors, the child study movement, led by G. S. Hall (1903), was the precursor of the psychological study of gifted children. The child study movement focused on the development of the individual child, and on the means by which parents and teachers could encourage the development of the child's full potential. Lewis Terman's longitudinal study, *Genetic Studies of Genius*, grew out of this movement. This study was unique in its ambitiousness—it began in 1921 and continues today, having followed the gifted from childhood to old age. It was also unique in its comprehensiveness; it explored the social and psychological as well as the intellectual development of gifted individuals. The Terman sample, as mentioned earlier, was probably biased in the direction of environmentally advantaged, teacher-favored children. It is not surprising that Terman concluded that gifted children are well adjusted and need little in the way of special guidance services (Terman, 1925). It was also the case that Terman and his colleagues were determined to lay to rest the popular notion at that time that genius was associated with sickliness, instability, and social awkwardness. Unfortunately, in going so far to disprove this stereotype, Terman created a new myth of the gifted child as almost a super-person: invariably healthier, stronger, more socially adept, and popular than the average child. Myers and Pace as well as many others (Webb, Meckstroth, & Tolan, 1982; Whitmore, 1980) believe that this new myth may have led to the neglect of gifted individuals by psychologists and counselors for many decades afterwards.

Unlike Terman, Leta Hollingworth (1926, 1942) found good reason to believe that gifted children need specialized guidance and counseling. Working with highly gifted students in the Speyer School at Columbia University, Hollingworth found that adjustment problems are evident in children with IQs over 150 and that higher IQs are associated with even greater difficulties in social and emotional adjustment. Hollingworth's case studies of highly gifted students show great psychological insight into and compassion for young people whose extreme intellectual abilities lead to academic, social, and emotional problems. Hollingworth depicted gifted children as struggling with boredom in classrooms where their curiosity and intellectual drive is unappreciated. She described the difficulties gifted children experience in peer relationships, where they are often shunned by their same-age peers because of their unusual interests and talents as well as by older children because of their size and occasional lack of similar emotional maturity. Hollingworth also clarified the problems gifted students encounter in finding their place in the world. Cynical attitudes arise from the helplessness a gifted child feels when he or she can understand a societal problem but cannot do anything about it; this is a poor beginning for a search for a meaningful adult life. Hollingworth also touched upon the fact that too many academic and career options also lead to helplessness and indecision.

After Leta Hollingworth, a long hiatus occurred in the interests of psychologists and counselors in bright students. Although a few scholars wrote about the psychology of gifted students in the 1940s and 1950s (Witty, 1940; Strang, 1951), no concerted efforts were made to develop counseling or guidance strategies for gifted students until the late 1950s.

The influence of both Lewis Terman and Frank Parsons, the founder of vocational guidance, were important to the establishment of the first Guidance Laboratory for Superior Students at The University of Wisconsin. John Rothney, founder of the Wisconsin Guidance Laboratory for Superior Students, had studied with colleagues of both of these scholars. For the first time, principles of vocational guidance were applied to the special case of gifted students. The Guidance Laboratory for Superior Students was a research-through-service program; gifted students from local schools received career guidance and participated in a variety of assessment procedures aimed at increasing knowledge about the counseling needs of this population. The Guidance Laboratory for Superior Students at The University of Wisconsin, later named Guidance Institute for Talented Students (GIFTS), was directed by Marshall Sanborn, Nicholas Colangelo, and Phillip Perrone. Until its closing in 1984, it was the major source of information on counseling and guiding gifted students.

The work of GIFTS was carried on, however, at two other counseling laboratories: the Guidance Laboratory for Gifted and Talented at the University of Nebraska, and the Counseling Laboratory for Talent Development at The University of Iowa, which I established in 1982 and 1986, respectively. The Guidance Laboratory for Gifted and Talented, now directed by Collie Conoley, is a program of UN-L's Educational Psychology Department. The Counseling Laboratory for Talent Development, which I direct, is a program of the Connie Belin National Center for Gifted Education. In addition to these centers, which emphasize career counseling for gifted adolescents and young adults, the Supporting Emotional Needs of the Gifted (SENG) program at Wright State University provides individual and group counseling for a wide variety of social and emotional difficulties. Directed by James T. Webb, this center was first established by a fund set up by the parents of Dallas Egbert, a highly gifted adolescent whose suicide in 1981 prompted national interest in the emotional needs of gifted students.

As interest in the counseling needs of gifted students grows, more training programs are allowing counselors to engage in practical experiences with such students. A new generation of graduate students in education and counseling are taking the initiative by doing research in the area of counseling needs of the gifted and talented. This book is an outgrowth of research and practice at the various guidance laboratories and the experiences of many psychologists and educators who work with gifted students in helping them to plan their education and their life's work.

## Overview of the Book

This handbook is organized as a practical guide to the counselor working with gifted students. It should be noted that throughout this book the word "gifted" is meant to include both "gifted" and "talented." Occasionally, "talented" is used to denote the possession of specific abilities. The first chapter, "The Counselor as Talent Scout: Identifying Gifted Students," takes up the issue of identifying gifts. The counselor is encouraged to seek ways not only of assisting schools in their formal identification processes for gifted and talented programs, but also discovering the gifts and talents among all students with whom they work. In this chapter, intelligence testing, achievement testing, and other means of identifying special talents are described. Suggestions are given to the counselor for discovering behaviors associated with various talents. Finally, ideas for nurturing and developing those talents are provided.

Chapter 2, "Academic Guidance and the Curriculum," represents a joint effort by myself and contributor Kirk Hallowell. Kirk Hallowell, assistant professor at Western Illinois University, and an experienced counselor of the gifted, contributed his theory of academic guidance, and coauthored an overview of various curriculum approaches commonly used with gifted and talented students. The thrust of this chapter is not the education of gifted students but rather the counseling and guidance implications of various commonly used approaches to teaching gifted students. Each approach to educating gifted students carries with it particular advantages for the student's adjustment and sometimes a few difficulties related to adjustment. This chapter shows how counselors can work with teachers and administrators to ensure that gifted programs are sufficiently challenging and supportive for bright students.

Chapter 3, "Counseling the Underachieving Gifted Student," explores a special case of academic guidance—the guidance of students whose performance in a classroom does not match their abilities as measured by intelligence tests, achievement tests, or past academic performance. The controversy over the definition of underachievement is discussed, and a model for creating hypotheses about underachievement is presented. Means of diagnosing underachievement and specific counseling strategies are offered.

Chapter 4, "College Planning for Gifted Students," approaches the dilemma of finding the right college for the gifted student by answering the most commonly asked questions about college planning. The year-by-year planning schedule for college decision making, developed by Sandra Berger of the ERIC Clearinghouse on Handicapped and Gifted Children, is summarized here as well.

Chapter 5, "Career Counseling for Gifted and Talented Students," describes the major problems in career decision making bright students encounter. The difficulties of being "multipotential"—having too many career options—and the misunderstood case of the "early emerger"— the child whose career goal is precociously focused—are discussed. This chapter suggests how career education and career counseling can ensure that gifted students live up to their potential. More important, however, than living up to intellectual potential is that gifted students develop a sense of purpose in life. This chapter shows how career development can become the search for meaning rather than simply the search for an occupation.

Chapter 6, "Counseling Gifted and Talented Girls," describes the special problems gifted girls encounter in their academic and career development. How counselors can help teachers to educate gifted girls more equitably is one emphasis of the chapter. Another is what counselors themselves can do to raise the aspirations of gifted girls and to ensure that bright girls and women achieve their dreams and goals.

Chapter 7, "Psychological Adjustment of Gifted Students," explores the research on the psychological adjustment of the gifted and talented as well as the specific psychological problems that may interact with giftedness. Adjustment is related to gender, age, educational placement, and talent area. Students in particular talent areas do seem to have psychological problems related to their gifts; counselors may need to understand the adjustment disorder fully. In addition, some psychological problems, such as stress reactions and depression, seem to appear among students in all talent categories. The unique plight of the gifted perfectionist is given special attention in this chapter. Bibliotherapy, a technique of helping gifted students through books, is explained and highlighted by an annotated reading list prepared by contributor Stephen Schroeder-Davis.

The final chapter, "Counseling Gifted Students: Techniques That Work," shows how guidance services can be designed and how the counselor can learn effective techniques for helping gifted students. Ways in which the counselor can become an advocate for gifted students is an important focus of this chapter. Resources for counselors who wish to help gifted students to make academic and career choices and to seek the support they need are included.

So much needs to be said about bright students, and making decisions about what to include in a book like this is a difficult process. Chapters, and whole books, need to be written on topics such as gifted children at risk, minority gifted students, and the gifted child in the family; information about these concerns is included within most of the chapters in this book. *A Handbook for Counseling the Gifted and Talented* is only a modest gathering of research and effective practices with gifted students; but it represents what I hope is a useful beginning for the counselor who wishes to learn about and work with this fascinating group of students.

## References

Hall, G. S. (1903). Child study at Clark University. *American Journal of Psychology, 14,* 96–106.

Hollingworth, L. S. (1926). *Gifted children: Their nature and nurture.* New York: Macmillan.

Hollingworth, L. S. (1942). *Children above 180 IQ, Stanford Binet*. New York: World Book.

Myers, R. S., & Pace, T. M. (1986). Counseling gifted and talented students: Historical perspectives and contemporary issues. *Journal of Counseling and Development, 64*, 548–551.

Strang, R. (1951). Mental hygiene of gifted children. In P. Witty (Ed.), *The gifted child* (pp. 131–162). Boston: American Association for Gifted Children.

Terman, L. M. (1925). Mental and physical traits of a thousand gifted children. In L. M. Terman (Ed.), *Genetic studies of genius* (Vol. 1). Stanford, CA: Stanford University Press.

Webb, J. T., Meckstroth, E. A., & Tolan, S. S. (1982). *Guiding the gifted child*. Columbus, OH: Ohio Psychology Publishing.

Whitmore, J. R. (1980). *Giftedness, conflict, and underachievement*. Boston: Allyn & Bacon.

Witty, P. (1940). Some considerations in the education of gifted children. *Educational Administration and Supervision, 26*, 512–521.

# The Counselor as Talent Scout: Identifying Gifted Students

How do you know which students are gifted? Most counselors respond by saying, "I look at the list I've been given." Because most counselors work in junior and senior high schools, the formal identification of gifted students is usually a *fait accompli* by the time counselors meet the students. Counselors are seldom involved in their school's or district's identification process. They don't sit on identification committees, and their expertise is usually not consulted. Many are not even given a list of students who have qualified for gifted education, and frequently no notation is made on the student's record.

Counselors may prefer to leave the identification of gifted students up to school psychologists and gifted educators. Despite the fact that counselors do have psychometric knowledge and test interpretation skills, they often believe that intelligence testing is beyond their scope. Therefore, they may not understand the basis upon which a student has been labeled as gifted, and may not be able to use the results of intelligence and achievement tests effectively in helping students. Even more unfortunate is the fact that a great many counselors suspect that the identification methods used in their school or district are not the most sound, but feel unable or unwilling to offer criticism or advice.

It is often the counselor who knows the gifted student as an individual, however. It is the counselor with whom the bright student has shared goals and dreams and analyzed weaknesses and strengths. There are counselors who look at their clients and see not just the girl who is applying for science camp, but the future physicist; not just the lonely, creative boy, but the future writer. These counselors are the true "talent scouts" for our society, and they should take an active role in helping schools to identify gifted students.

## Problems With Identification Practices

As a major national survey of identification practices showed (Richert, 1985), the process of identifying gifted students is carried out poorly in most of the nation's schools. According to Richert, there is a "distressing gap between research and its application to equitable identification procedures" (p. 4). The major problems with identification practices are:

1. There is a misunderstanding or lack of application of the broad federal definition.
2. Tests are used in ways they were not intended and for inappropriate populations.
3. Biased tests and procedures violate educational equity and screen out disadvantaged students.
4. Multiple criteria are combined in ways that are statistically unsound, or multiple criteria are not being used as intended.
5. Instruments and procedures are used at inappropriate stages of identification.

It is important to take each of these problems into consideration in turn to show how they have affected gifted students.

The federal definition of giftedness was developed by the U.S. Office of Education (as quoted in Marland, 1972, p. 1):

Gifted and talented students are those identified by professionally qualified persons, who by virtue of outstanding abilities, are capable of high performance. These are children who require differentiated educational programs and/or services beyond those normally provided by "regular school program" in order to realize their contributions to self and society.

Children with "demonstrated" and/or "potential" high performance in the following areas: (a) general intellectual ability, (b) specific academic aptitude, (c) creative or productive thinking, (d) leadership ability, and (e) psychomotor ability.

The misunderstandings of the federal definition often involve assuming that gifted children must have *all* the above abilities rather than just one in order to be considered gifted; believing that this federal statement narrows the definition of the gifted, when it actually is intended to broaden it; and assuming that "gifted" and "talented" are separate populations, when the terms are overlapping and usage is often interchangeable. When "gifted and talented" is used, it is an inclusive phrase meant to indicate a broader group than just the academically gifted. The federal definition is useful for the states, cities, and school districts that need a comprehensive, inclusive definition. It is *not* meant to regulate any particular school's gifted program; in fact, few schools could implement the entire definition because the programming such a definition would require would be beyond the scope of most schools. The only use for a definition is the identification of students for specific programming; it is unlikely that any one gifted program could meet the needs of all students who could fit the federal definition. The federal definition implies the desirability of multiple criteria for giftedness *and* multiple programs, *not* one amorphous, general identification strategy linked to one equally shapeless program. A particular school's identification procedure should be based on the gifts and talents of the children in that school and the resources of the school for nurturing particular abilities.

The second problem with current identification practices is inappropriate test use, which is widespread. Some common examples are:

- Using cutoff scores from achievement tests that are meant to be measures of a group's educational progress to select individuals for gifted programs. This is particularly a problem in the lower grades, where individual students' scores on achievement tests are highly variable.
- Using an instrument that measures only one, or a few, aspects of a trait to predict overall presence of that trait. For example, the Torr-

ance Tests of Creative Thinking measure fluency, flexibility, originality, and elaboration in thought processes; but they do not measure
motivation, commitment, and persistence, which also may be critical
to productive creativity. It is inappropriate to label a child "creatively
gifted" based on scores from this test alone.

- Assuming that a test designed to measure one desirable trait measures
  others for which it was not designed. Frequently, IQ tests are believed
  to be measures of "social giftedness," leadership, and other desirable traits.
- Using a single test in isolation, rather than a battery of tests and
  other observations. Even the best tests of general intellectual ability
  such as the WISC-R and Stanford-Binet need to be corroborated
  with other evidence.
- Using intelligence tests to predict both divergent, or creative thinking
  as well as convergent, or logical thinking, when they are designed
  to measure mainly convergent thinking.

The third problem, test bias, involves tests that were normed on pre-
dominantly White, upper-middle-class children to predict the academic
abilities of minority and disadvantaged populations. Most intelligence
tests and achievement tests are normed on disproportionately White, high
socioeconomic status groups, although newer revisions of the older tests,
such as the 4th edition of the Stanford-Binet, and newer tests, such as
the Kaufman ABC, attempt to include more diversity in their standard-
ization samples.

The issue of test bias is highly controversial. Test makers claim freedom
from bias and the use of appropriate safeguards, whereas educational
psychologists find instances in which items are oriented toward White,
male, middle-class experiences as well as evidence that many tests of
intellectual potential underpredict, or underestimate, the actual achievement of minorities. It is clear, however, that Blacks, Hispanics, and
Native Americans are greatly underrepresented in gifted education classes. According to McKenzie (1986), identification procedures that use
standardized achievement tests and intelligence scales reinforce social
inequalities and miss some of the most promising students.

The fourth problem, inappropriate combinations of multiple criteria,
is related to two flawed practices. The first is the "cosmetic" use of
multiple selection criteria. An example of cosmetic use is administering

a number of instruments and gathering other observations such as teacher checklists in addition to an intelligence test, when in the final selection everything but the intelligence test is ignored. The other flawed practice is combining several test scores or assigning points to a variety of measures in a way that gives equal weight to all of the measures, or inappropriate weights to some of the measures. Where measures are combined, careful statistical procedures should be used so that the resulting prediction formula is sound.

Finally, the problem of using instruments at inappropriate stages often reflects a misunderstanding of the basic fact that intelligence tests are meant to predict future academic behavior, not to measure achievement or to evaluate the effects of an academic program. Sternberg (1982) gave the example of a student who was admitted to a teacher's college despite a low score on the Miller Analogies Test but performed with distinction in her classes. Before she was allowed to graduate, however, she was required to retake the Miller Analogies Test and raise her score. Sternberg lamented that, "The predictor had somehow come to surpass the criterion for importance!" (p. 160).

In addition to this blatantly inappropriate use of a test of intellectual potential, there are many other examples of tests used either too early or too late to identify students for a gifted education program effectively. Most intelligence and achievement test scores are somewhat unstable for young children under 8 or 9 years of age; administering a test early and only once may give an inadequate measure of an individual child's potential. Administering a standardized intelligence test such as the Stanford-Binet in high school is an example of testing too late; by this age, there is plenty of evidence of academic achievement. The best predictor of future academic achievement is past academic achievement (grades and achievement test scores), not intelligence tests.

In summary, a great many problems exist in the gifted education identification procedures used in the nation's schools. There is much room for improvement, and there is a place for the counselor's expertise. The counselor should be familiar with standardized instruments used for identification for gifted education and with a variety of identification strategies now in use in the schools. The identification strategies presented here are examples of strategies based on current popular models. The instruments introduced here and reviewed in the Resources section at the end of the book are those that are the most widely used.

## Standardized Instruments Used in the Identification of Gifted Students

The most common type of instrument used in the identification of gifted students is the individual intelligence test. A recent survey of school psychologists found that the three most frequently used intelligence tests were the Wechsler Intelligence Scale for Children-Revised (WISC-R) (Wechsler, 1974), the Stanford-Binet Intelligence Scale (3rd & 4th editions) (Terman & Merrill, 1960; Thorndike, Hagen, Sattler, & Delaney, 1986), and the Kaufman Assessment Battery for Children (K-ABC) (Kaufman & Kaufman, 1983). The WISC-R was the overwhelming first choice (Klausmeier, Mishra, & Maker, 1987). Nevertheless, many experts (Silverman, Chitwood, & Waters, 1986; Stanley, 1984) consider the Stanford-Binet to be the best instrument for identifying the general intellectual ability required by most gifted programs. These two instruments are very similar and highly correlated.

Other instruments school psychologists name as being commonly used in the identification of gifted students include achievement tests such as the Stanford Achievement Test (Gardner, Rudman, Karlsen, & Merwin, 1982), the Peabody Individual Achievement Test (Dunn & Markwardt, 1970), and the Wide Range Achievement Test (Jastak & Jastak, 1978); a combined ability, achievement, and interest test called the Woodcock-Johnson Psycho-Educational Battery (Woodcock & Johnson, 1977); and a creativity test, the Torrance Tests of Creative Thinking (Torrance, 1974). Recent literature on the identification of gifted minority and disadvantaged students has focused on the Raven Progressive Matrices (Baska, 1986) and the System of Multicultural Pluralistic Assessment (Mercer & Lewis, 1978). The use of out-of-level achievement tests such as the Scholastic Aptitude Tests for identifying students with specific academic aptitudes has been a successful practice with junior high students participating in Talent Search programs (Stanley, 1984; Van Tassel-Baska, 1986).

Finally, a set of standardized instruments designed for testing multiple intellectual abilities, based on Guilford's (1967) Structure of Intellect Model, the Structure of Intellect-Screening Form for the Gifted (SOI-SFG) (Meeker & Meeker, 1979), is gaining popularity as an identification procedure for gifted students, but, so far, there has not been strong evidence to support its usefulness (O'Tuel, Ward, & Rawl, 1983). Detailed descriptions and critiques of these most widely used instruments are included in the Resources section at the end of this book.

## Identification Strategies

Although a wide variety of identification strategies is described in the gifted education literature and promoted by the developers, most schools in the United States have some hybrid form of identification strategy that takes into account the population characteristics, the resources available, the expertise of the program administrators, and the political climate. Therefore, a school with a textbook example of an identification plan would be rare. The formal identification strategies on which most schools base their variants include the Revolving Door Identification Model (Renzulli, Reis, & Smith, 1981), the Structure of Intellect Model, the Talent Search Model (Stanley, 1984; Van Tassel-Baska, 1986), and the Pyramid Model.

## Revolving Door Identification Model

The Revolving Door Identification Model (Renzulli et al., 1981) begins with the selection of a "talent pool" of about 20% of the school population; students may be screened for the talent pool by traditional techniques: intelligence tests, aptitude tests, and achievement tests. However, because giftedness is considered to be a combination of intelligence, task commitment, and creativity, creativity tests, teacher checklists, parent nomination forms, and students' self-evaluations are also used. Students are identified for the purpose of participating in a variety of enrichment activities: Type I enrichment, which includes such activities as special speakers, projects, field trips, and seminars; Type II enrichment, which provides such activities as research skills and group problem solving; and Type III enrichment, which allows individual research and eventually leads to reports and projects in areas of special interest.

Students who become interested in particular topics through Type I activities revolve into Type II to learn skills needed to pursue the investigations and problems of Type II enrichment. Students chosen for such programs are usually "generalists": young people with many moderately strong abilities. The frequent use of teacher checklists in the identification process may bias the selection in favor of students who tend to be well liked by teachers and who are well adjusted. Because creativity is often judged in terms of overt classroom behavior, selected students are often also those who are most expressive and outgoing. Because task commitment is often considered synonymous with the possession of good work habits, students selected by this process tend to be orderly, careful, and punctual in their work.

It is possible for a student of very high intelligence, (e.g., an IQ of 150), *not* to be selected through this process because of the emphasis on creativity and task commitment. It is also possible for a student with specific, extraordinary talent to be passed over.

## The Structure of Intellect Model

The SOI Model (Meeker & Meeker, 1979) is a diagnostic-prescriptive model in that it uses the Structure of Intellect-Learning Abilities Screening Form for Gifted (SOI-LA SFG) in order to "diagnose" strengths and weaknesses and then prescribe learning activities designed to nurture strengths and improve upon weaknesses. Children identified as gifted are those who receive high scores on the screening form, meaning that they display a variety of higher-order intellectual abilities. Because of the psychometric difficulties of the instrument, it is hard to say exactly what kinds of students are identified.

According to the test authors' research, this model is effective in identifying minority students. Because the SOI deemphasizes academic talent, it is likely that pools of children identified by this method possess talents other than, or in addition to, academic talent. Spatially-visually gifted and creatively gifted students are more likely to be selected by SOI identification procedures than by other procedures. It should also be noted that this method may lead to emphasizing students' weaknesses rather than strengths.

## Talent Search Model

The Talent Search Model (Stanley, 1984; Van Tassel-Baska, 1986) uses out-of-level testing in particular academic areas to identify academically talented students who can benefit by acceleration and other forms of intellectual challenge. The Talent Search Model, pioneered by Julian Stanley at Johns Hopkins University, now operates in four regions throughout the United States. All Talent Search programs were originally administered by universities. The Talent Search Model is extremely focused. For example, it concentrates on junior high students who take the SAT (and now the ACT in some areas) in seventh grade. Students who score at or above the mean for high school seniors on at least one subscale are then invited to seek educational opportunities in their areas of talent at a wide variety of colleges and universities that provide accelerated and special classes.

Second, this identification model is extremely focused in that it does a few things well—that is, it identifies mathematically precocious or verbally precocious youth in order to provide appropriate education in math-related or verbally related areas. Students selected by the Talent Search method are therefore extremely talented in at least one academic area. Because academic talent is strongly associated with IQ, it is likely that these students also receive very high scores on intelligence measures and would be labeled "highly gifted."

These are students who can benefit a great deal from acceleration strategies; their ability to excel on standardized achievement instruments, which test for knowledge and reasoning abilities far beyond their grade level, usually indicates their competence to learn rapidly. Students identified by Talent Search techniques are not necessarily creative or socially gifted; however, follow-up studies of students identified by this method and educated accordingly show this group to be highly accomplished in late adolescence and young adulthood.

## The Pyramid Model

The Pyramid Model (Cox, Daniel, & Boston, 1985) is a recent, comprehensive identification and curriculum model. It is a synthesis of many existing approaches because it is based on an extensive survey of gifted education and on the research to date. The Pyramid Model calls for identification of many levels of talent. At the base of the pyramid are above-average students in a wide variety of talent areas who can benefit from enrichment in the classroom. At the next level are students who are most typically identified by the Revolving Door Identification Model. These students can benefit from a somewhat differentiated program or a pull-out enrichment program. At the next level are students whose abilities in particular talent areas or whose general abilities are so extreme that they warrant special classes in those areas; these are typically students who benefit from accelerative strategies. Finally, at the apex of the pyramid are students whose talents are so rare or extreme that they are best served by special placement such as science high schools, early admission to college, or fine arts institutes. The Pyramid Model holds promise as a flexible, comprehensive system of identification.

## How Counselors Can Participate in the Identification of Gifted Students

Counselors can help in the identification of gifted students in a variety of ways, according to their training and interests. The following are some suggested roles for the counselor in the identification process.

### Arriving at a Definition

- Facilitating a discussion of the types of definitions in current use: "What are we calling giftedness?"
- Facilitating a discussion of the values underlying each definition and the appropriateness of various definitions to the local community's values: "What does our definition of giftedness reflect about our community's values?"
- Explaining the importance of linking each component of the definition to valid, reliable instruments and accurate behavioral observations: "How do we know we are measuring abilities accurately?"
- Explaining the importance of linking the definition to academic programming: "Does identification as creative lead to creativity-based programs? Does identification as verbally gifted lead to a verbally challenging curriculum?" Or more facetiously, "Does the punishment fit the crime?"

### Instrument Selection

As consultants to gifted educators and administrators in the test selection process, counselors can share their expertise in the areas of psychological measurement and use of educational research. This should include:

- Explaining the concepts of test validity and reliability.
- Explaining the necessity of multiple measures of behavior.
- Providing an understanding of test limitations.
- Demonstrating the use of *Buros Mental Measurements Yearbook* and *Tests in Print*.

- Familiarizing educators and administrators with the Council for Exceptional Children—The Association for the Gifted standards that apply to identification.
- Explaining concepts of validity and interrater reliability of teacher and parent behavior checklists.
- Helping determine an appropriate combination of measures, and suggest statistically valid ways of combining scores.
- Providing references or copies of articles concerning the use of the chosen instruments with gifted students.

## Identifying and Nurturing Talents

The counselor can be most effective as a talent scout if he or she attempts to discover students' talents in specific areas. This kind of discovery is most likely to occur during counseling sessions about academic or career planning. A student whose specific, extraordinary talent for writing or playing the flute or doing theoretical mathematics may otherwise have been obscured by an average grade point average or average composite scores is likely to be discovered only by a particularly attentive teacher or counselor. According to Gardner's (1983) theory of multiple intelligences, a great many talents exist in isolation from other abilities. Psychologists and gifted educators are only just beginning to contemplate ways in which specific talents can be measured. Although the traditional academic apttitudes such as verbal and mathematical skills have been associated with achievement tests and other measures, most nontraditional areas of talent often have had no corresponding instrument. In this century, psychologists have attempted to devise measures of talent such as musical ability and artistic ability by analyzing the components of those abilities that seem to be related to success. These instruments have never been widely used, perhaps because there have not been much data to support their ability to identify and predict accomplishment.

Attempts to measure specific talent often go beyond measuring performance of tasks related to the talent area. For example, Nicholas Colangelo and I and our student colleagues have been developing the Iowa Inventiveness Inventory, a measure of mechanical inventiveness. This instrument actually measures the degree to which students possess the personality characteristics, habits, and life experiences that are similar to those of eminent inventors.

It is unlikely that at any time in the near future instruments will exist that can accurately identify students whose specific, extraordinary talents can lead to eminence in a particular area of performance. Nevertheless, a perusal of the research in particular talent areas will show that particular student behavior, and in some cases, student performance on school tasks and tests, is a good indicator of specific abilities. Therefore, the following list has been constructed by summarizing the research findings in each area of talent. This list is based on Gardner's theory of multiple intelligences and describes behaviors associated with verbal, mathematical, spatial-visual, musical, and leadership talents.

## VERBAL GIFTEDNESS

*How It Might Be Discovered*

*What the Counselor Can Do*

The student . . .
Is an avid reader whose knowledge of literature in general or some area of literature (mysteries, drama, science fiction) is much more extensive than that of other students.

OR

Is a gifted writer whose poetry or prose is more sophisticated or more moving than the works of others of a similar age.

OR

Has excellent grades in language arts and English courses.

OR

Has a sense of humor that often leads to the role of the comedian or wit.

OR

Has a gift for learning languages.

OR

Has high scores on the Stanford-Binet, the WISC-R Verbal, the Miller Analogies Test, or other tests of verbal aptitude.

Encourage participation in summer programs, creative writing, journalism, speech and debate, drama, foreign languages.

Encourage entry into writing contests, speech contests, theatre arts competitions.

Seek opportunities for publication through literary magazines, newspapers, and book publishers.

Explore colleges and universities with strong creative writing programs (or journalism, theater, or foreign language).

Seek a mentor in local community or at a college or university.

OR

Has high scores on verbal achievement tests taken out of level, for example, scores above the mean for high school seniors on the SAT-V while still in junior high.

## SPATIAL-VISUAL GIFTEDNESS

*How It Might Be Discovered*

*What the Counselor Can Do*

The student . . .
Draws models or builds with technical skill and imagination.

Help student find advanced instruction in his or her talent area, such as a college painting class.

OR

Surpasses peers in ability to create cartoons, paintings, sculpture, or architectural or mechanical models.

Arrange a mentorship or apprenticeship with an appropriate professional, such as an architect or mechanic.

OR

Has high scores on WISC-R Performance scale, the Raven Progressive Matrices, or other test of spatial-visual reasoning.

Encourage participation in fine arts camps and special arts programs.

Help student to discover the career ladder in his or her area of talent, e.g., for visual arts, building a portfolio and seeking shows for one's work.

OR

Has high scores on the Figural section of the Torrance Tests of Creative Thinking.

Help student locate appropriate postsecondary education at an art institute, college, or university with strong art programs, or in the case of technical or mechanical talent, architecture or mechanical engineering programs.

OR

Has excellent grades in art, shop, mechanical drawing, or other courses requiring spatial-visual ability.

## MUSICAL GIFTEDNESS

*How It Might Be Discovered*

*What the Counselor Can Do*

The student . . .
Sings or plays an instrument beautifully and seems to love performing.

Help student find individualized lessons with an appropriate teacher.

OR

Surpasses peers in musical knowledge and sophistication in general or in specific areas such as jazz, classical, or rock.

OR

Has unusual musical abilities such as "perfect pitch," or musical memory.

OR

Has excellent grades in music.

Encourage participation in school, community, and church music groups.

Encourage participation in music camps and summer programs.

Help student with "audition skills" such as progressive relaxation to overcome performance anxiety.

Explore institutes of music, colleges, and universities with well-known choirs, bands, or orchestras.

## MATHEMATICAL GIFTEDNESS

*How It Might Be Discovered*

*What the Counselor Can Do*

The student . . .
Is a "natural" mathematician, able to do unusually complex computational tasks in his or her head.

OR

Has advanced much farther than peers in math knowledge and understanding.

OR

Has excellent grades in math courses.

OR

Does very well on arithmetic-quantitative reasoning portions of intelligence tests.

OR

Has high scores on math achievement tests taken out of level, for example, scores at the mean for high school seniors while still in junior high.

Help the student to accelerate math learning through special classes, advanced courses, or by skipping ahead in math.

Encourage entry and participation in summer math camps and similar programs.

Encourage entry into math contests such as "Math Counts" and computer competitions.

Explore colleges and universities with strong math departments (or physics, engineering, computer science, statistics, or other math-related field).

Seek a mentor in math from a college or university.

## INTERPERSONAL GIFTEDNESS

*How It Might Be Discovered*

*What the Counselor Can Do*

The student . . .

Has held a variety of formal leadership positions.

OR

Frequently rises to positions of informal leadership.

OR

Surpasses peers in ability to listen, communicate, and persuade.

OR

Has high scores on verbal scales of WISC-R or Stanford-Binet.

OR

Has excellent grades in speech, debate, rhetoric, and other courses requiring communication and persuasion skills.

OR

Has high scores on ACT Social Studies subtest.

Encourage formal study of leadership through courses on such topics as group dynamics and organizational development.

Encourage participation in summer leadership camps and conferences.

Encourage participation in community, state, and national organizations where leadership skills can be nurtured.

Explore colleges and universities with strong programs in such fields as political science, business, higher education, law, sociology, or psychology.

## Summary

Counselors can take an active role in the process of identifying gifted students. By understanding instruments and strategies, assisting in developing a definition of giftedness, and assisting in selecting instruments, the counselor can lend technical expertise. More important, by using his or her own personal knowledge of students' strengths as well as skillful observation and surmise, the counselor can be a true talent scout.

## References

Baska, L. (1986). The use of the Raven Advanced Progressive Matrices for the selection of magnet junior high school students. Special Issue: The I.Q. Controversy. *Roeper Review, 8*(3), 181–184.

Cox, J., Daniel, N., & Boston, B. (1985). *Educating able learners: Programs and promising practices.* Austin, TX: University of Texas Press.

Dunn, L. M., & Markwardt, F. C., Jr. (1970). *Peabody Individual Achievement Test.* Circle Pines, MN: American Guidance Service.

Gardner, E. F., Rudman, H. C., Karlsen, B., & Merwin, J. C. (1982). *Stanford Measurement Series-Stanford Achievement Test* (7th ed.). New York: Psychological Corporation.

Gardner, H. (1983). *Frames of mind.* New York: Basic Books.

Guilford, J. P. (1967). *The nature of human intelligence.* New York: McGraw-Hill.

Jastak, J. F., & Jastak, S. (1978). *Wide Range Achievement Test.* Wilmington, DE: Jastak Associates.

Kaufman, A. S., & Kaufman, N. L. (1983). *Kaufman Assessment Battery for Children.* Circle Pines, MN: American Guidance Service.

Klausmeier, K. L., Mishra, S. P., & Maker, C. J. (1987). Identification of gifted learners: A national survey of assessment practices and training needs of school psychologists. *Gifted Child Quarterly, 31*(3), 135–137.

Marland, S. (1972). *Education of the gifted and talented.* Report to the Congress of the United States by the U.S. Commission of Education. Washington, DC: U.S. Government Printing Office.

McKenzie, J. A. (1986). The influence of identification practices, race and SES on the identification of gifted students. *Gifted Child Quarterly, 30,* 93–95.

Meeker, M., & Meeker, R. (1979). *SO screening form for gifted.* El Segundo, CA: SOI Institute.

Mercer, J. R., & Lewis, J. F. (1978). *System of multicultural pluralistic assessment.* San Antonio, TX: Psychological Corporation.

O'Tuel, F. S., Ward, M., & Rawl, R. K. (1983). The SOI as an identification tool for the gifted: Windfall or washout? *Gifted Child Quarterly, 27*(3), 126–134.

Renzulli, J. S., Reis, S. M., & Smith, L. H. (1981). *The Revolving Door Identification Model.* Mansfield, CT: Creative Learning Press.

Richert, E. S. (1985). The state of the art of identification of gifted students in the United States. *Gifted Education International, 3*(1), 47–51.

Silverman, L. K., Chitwood, D. G., & Waters, J. L. (1986). Young gifted children: Can parents identify giftedness? *Topics in Early Childhood Special Education, 6*(1), 23–38.

Stanley, J. C. (1984). Use of general and specific aptitude measures in identification: Some principles and certain cautions. *Gifted Child Quarterly, 28*(4), 177–180.

Sternberg, R. J. (1982). Lies we live by: Misapplication of tests in identifying the gifted. *Gifted Child Quarterly, 26*(4), 157–161.

Terman, L. M., & Merrill, M. A. (1960). *Revised Stanford-Binet Scale*. New York: Houghton-Mifflin.

Thorndike, R. L., Sattler, J. M., & Delaney, E. A. (1986). *Stanford-Binet Intelligence Scale, Fourth Edition*. Chicago: Riverside.

Torrance, E. P. (1974). *The Torrance tests of creative thinking: Norms-technical manual*. Bensenville, IL: Scholastic Testing Service.

Van Tassel-Baska, J. (1986). The use of aptitude tests for identifying the gifted: The talent search concept. *Roeper Review, 8*(3), 185–189.

Wechsler, D. (1974). *Wechsler Intelligence Scale for Children*. San Antonio, TX: Psychological Corporation.

Woodcock, R. W., & Johnson, M. B. (1977). *Woodcock-Johnson Psycho-Educational Battery*. Allen, TX: DLM Teaching Resources.

# Academic Guidance and the Curriculum

The counselor who sets out to establish a successful academic guidance program for talented students is beginning a challenging task. Scores of books and hundreds of articles have dealt with the design, implementation, and assessment of curricula, special programs, and guidance practices devised to meet the specific needs of gifted learners. Contributors to this literature represent the perspectives of numerous specializations in both education and psychology. Theories, based on varying assumptions and sometimes contradictory research evidence, abound. It is not surprising that the field of gifted education has been regularly criticized as lacking substantial and cohesive philosophical underpinnings (Ward, 1985).

Despite this complexity, the gifted education literature does include a wealth of vital information for counselors who want to help talented students make appropriate academic decisions. Although practices and recommendations are divergent, there is evidence that many of these approaches are successful in meeting the needs of gifted students. The task of the counselor is to review, interpret, synthesize, and integrate from these reports a cohesive framework that meets the specific population, environmental, and educational objectives for which the counselor is responsible. It is this process that makes the task so challenging. The purpose of this chapter is to assist the school counselor in taking the initial steps in this process.

As a resource for the counselor, there are four primary objectives of the chapter:

1. To familiarize the counselor with a set of theoretical themes that provide the basis for the appropriate academic guidance of gifted students.
2. To briefly summarize some of the major controversies typically encountered in gifted education and to illustrate the counselor's role as advocate in addressing these concerns.
3. To review a selection of curricular models currently employed in schools to meet the needs of gifted students.
4. To suggest guidance needs of gifted students based on the effects of various curricular models.

Although it is hoped that this chapter will serve as a starting place for the counselor who initiates a comprehensive academic guidance program for gifted students, this is only the beginning of the challenge. Further research and review of suggested materials as well as careful planning and implementation are essential to the development of a successful program.

## Theoretical Foundations

Certainly no single statement is capable of expressing the diversity of thought on what gifted students need to realize their academic potential. What is suggested here are three general descriptive terms which, as a group, begin to encompass common themes represented in the gifted literature. Although not all writers use these exact terms, they are consistent with the assumptions and findings of much of the field. These three terms are: *developmental, differential,* and *proactive.* Because each of these terms has grown to have its own set of meanings in different settings, a discussion of each term as it is used in the context of this chapter follows.

## Developmental

A primary characteristic of American educational research is its historical foundation in developmental psychology. Often cited is Piaget's interpretation of cognitive development as a universal and sequential process marked by defined stages and a predictable process of transition between stages. These views developed in turn from earlier scientific models of development that emerged from the natural sciences. Consistent with its historical evolution, the concept of "developmental" is used to refer to progressive changes that have been documented to take place in gifted learners. The following assertions have been supported by research in gifted education:

1. Through the process of physical and intellectual maturation, the characteristics, and consequently the needs, of gifted individuals change substantially over time. Successful programs will change with these needs.
2. This process of development includes universal patterns all people share. Because of this, it is possible to meet many needs of talented individuals through a general program of education.
3. Changes that take place in talented students are sequential and, to some degree, predictable. Therefore appropriate strategies of intervention can be developed in anticipation of specific needs as they arise.

These characteristics have two practical implications for a successful academic guidance program. First, and most important, the program must accommodate the sequential changes in intellectual and personal needs of gifted students. Goals and objectives for the academic planning of a gifted eighth grader will need to change substantially as that student progresses through high school. Second, although gifted individuals will vary widely in pace and nature of academic development, several commonalities of development warrant a general plan of educational alternatives. Such a plan must be flexible enough to meet individual differences. Thus, the necessity of a central framework for academic planning does not necessarily conflict with the need for individualization of that program.

## Differential

The term *differential* has become the key concept in curriculum development and academic planning for gifted students. This term is principally used to describe the intellectual characteristics of gifted learners. This use is supported by an extended history of research indicating that gifted learners are not only quantitatively different (learning more and learning faster), but also qualitatively different (learning in different modes and at greater depth) than their typical peers. In addition to showing differences in learning, current research also indicates that gifted learners have unique concerns in social, emotional, and vocational development. With this evidence in mind, educators have sought to tailor programs to meet the differential needs of highly able students.

A second use of the term *differential* is to refer to differences among groups within the general gifted and talented population. Several new trends in gifted education research indicate that giftedness is a complex and multifaceted concept applicable to diverse subgroups of students. Each of these groups has characteristically specific needs in terms of academic development. Examples of these trends include Howard Gardner's (1983) theory of multiple intelligences and Sternberg and Davidson's (1986) triarchic model of intelligence. In addition, growing attention has been given to the special needs of specific groups of gifted students including the underachieving, learning disabled, disadvantaged, culturally diverse, and physically disabled gifted.

For the school counselor, the idea of differential education for the gifted has implications for each of these two levels of meaning. First, educational options need to meet the intellectual demands that define gifted students as a whole. The most central concern represented in the literature in this respect is to provide appropriate intellectual challenge. Substantive evidence indicates that capable learners learn most effectively when appropriately challenged and tend to become bored and frustrated when the pace and complexity of material is below their ability. The second meaning of differential, referring to differences among groups within the gifted, indicates that educators of the gifted must accommodate a growing number of academic objectives and concerns associated with new groups of gifted students as they are identified.

## Proactive

Despite its becoming a standard buzzword in the areas of education, management, and human relations training, the term *proactive* effectively describes attributes of successful practices for gifted learners. *Proactive*, as it is used here, refers not so much to the content of a particular program, but instead to the process by which the program is conceived and implemented. A proactive approach to gifted and talented education begins with the needs and concerns of the student as an individual, not as a reaction to external stimuli. The first concern of the proactive counselor lies in helping the student, not in placating parents or school officials.

Buescher (1987) stressed a second aspect of a proactive approach. In a model for counseling gifted adolescents, Buescher effectively differentiated between proactive approaches to guiding gifted learners as preventative as opposed to intervening and remedial. A reactive approach centers on the need to respond to problems in a gifted student's development. Although such intervention strategies are necessary, Buescher argued that it is preferable to develop strategies that meet special needs of gifted students *before* problems arise.

A proactive stance to guiding talented students may indeed be one of the most difficult aspects of a successful program. The proactive process begins with developing a clear understanding of the unique educational needs and aspirations of talented students as individuals. Effective programs have used standardized testing, assessment worksheets, and individual counseling interviews to accomplish this objective. Certainly this kind of individual attention is not easy when guidance counselors are assigned caseloads of 300 to 500 students. Proactive academic guidance may be nearly impossible if counselors are also expected to deal with mental health concerns, substance abuse, and unwanted pregnancies in addition to academic advocacy.

Another threat to a proactive approach arises from the common political environment in which many schools are immersed. In a period when schools are changing in response to national, state, and local agendas on educational quality, there is a natural tendency to focus program goals on what will be institutionally advantageous. Capable counselors must be aware of and assimilate external influences into a successful academic guidance program, but the core mission of the program must revolve around the individual needs of each student. In some cases, this means that counselors may have to make recommendations for the good of the student that are not necessarily popular with other parties.

## Summary

The terms, *developmental*, *differential*, and *proactive* provide the philosophical basis for a successful guidance program designed to meet the needs of talented students. The developmental and differential needs of gifted students have been defined by common themes emerging from a large and complex history of research. This research has diversified to focus on several distinct subpopulations within a general gifted population. The need for a proactive approach centers on the understanding that appropriate guidance begins with the specific, individual needs of each student and that these needs should be met before problems are encountered. These key concepts will now be used as a basis for discussing and evaluating alternatives in building a successful academic guidance program for gifted students.

At this point, more questions have been raised than answered about the content of a successful academic guidance program for gifted students. How will a successful program meet the changing needs of the gifted as they progress through high school? How will a central program meet the special needs of different groups of gifted students? Finally, what resources and alternatives are necessary to meet these special needs? The remainder of this chapter is devoted to answering these questions.

## Curriculum Choices for the Gifted Student

It is unfortunate that in the myriad of tasks typically assigned to school counselors, involvement in the selection and design of academic curricula is not a common job expectation. School counselors are expected to coordinate personal, educational, and vocational counseling for students and consult with teachers and parents about these processes. Counselors will inevitably deal with issues related to academic curricula, but they are rarely expected to be involved in academic curricular development. Counselors need to develop a closer alliance with administrators and classroom teachers in designing the classroom experience.

As an advocate for the appropriate education of students in general, the counselor should be prepared to develop defensible recommendations for gifted students. In order for the counselor to function effectively in the role of advocate, the counselor must develop an understanding of the issues and alternatives currently associated with gifted education. To begin with, a counselor can anticipate a few major controversies in any attempt to alter the curriculum to meet the needs of talented students. Counselors should be familiar with these controversial issues and understand the rationale and research evidence used to support conflicting viewpoints. Second, counselors should become familiar with some of the major curriculum models that are commonly used to meet the differential needs of gifted learners. With this information, the counselor will be far better equipped to participate in curriculum planning and to deal effectively with problems associated with differential education of gifted students.

## Controversies in Gifted Education

From its inception in American education, differential treatment of high-ability students has included controversial issues. Conflicting viewpoints emerge from two primary sources: one, criticisms of basic tenets of gifted education from those outside of the field and, two, controversies over theory and practice within the field. Any counselor who decides to take an active role in the design and implementation of differential curricula for gifted learners should anticipate and prepare to encounter these issues. A successful counselor will understand the nature of these debates and be versed in the defense of a justifiable position.

Controversies arise over almost any aspect of gifted education, from identification to life-span, developmental issues. Over the years, many of these controversies have erupted in heated debates in educational literature, political struggles in legislatures and school districts, and legal action in the court systems. Although these issues are far too numerous and complex to discuss here in detail, three issues related to curriculum development for secondary gifted students will be reviewed. These issues include the elitism, homogeneous grouping, and the enrichment versus acceleration controversies. Counselors who encounter one or more of these issues are encouraged to review the references cited in this section.

### The Elitism Controversy

Perhaps the most prevalent criticism of gifted education from outside the field is the charge that differential education promotes a sense of elitism among students who receive special educational opportunities. Advocates of this view hold that identification, labeling, and special treatment of a group of students will invariably result in their developing the attitude that they are superior to other students. Not only is labeling seen as potentially destructive to the students who are identified as gifted, but also to the other students who are not identified and consequently sense that they are intellectually second rate. The argument on these lines follows the self-fulfilling prophesy criticism of educational tracking: Students who are not identified as gifted are less likely to aspire to higher achievement.

The most common response to this criticism centers on the argument for egalitarian treatment of students in providing appropriate educational experiences. Proponents of this view often quote Thomas Jefferson: "There is nothing more unequal than the equal treatment of unequal people." Although the egalitarian argument is widely held in defense of gifted education, some educators still question the validity of excluding students who might benefit from the kind of programming made available to gifted students. Renzulli's Revolving Door Identification Model provides at least a partial answer to this concern in making gifted programming accessible to a larger pool of students than that defined by an arbitrary identification cutoff (Renzulli, Reis, & Smith, 1981). Although Myers and Ridl (1981) accept the idea of egalitarianism in education, they warn that classifying students by ability may result in an "academic caste system" that will reflect socioeconomic and possibly racial segregation.

There is considerable concern over the specter of elitism in gifted education, but there is little documented evidence of elitist attitudes among educators of the gifted or gifted students themselves. In extensive interviews with gifted students, Delisle (1984) found that gifted students did not express any sense of superiority over their typical peers. In addition, reports focusing on students' reaction to the label of "giftedness" did not reflect attitudes of elitism among gifted students toward their peers or siblings (Colangelo & Brower, 1987). Undoubtedly, elitist attitudes do exist among some gifted students, but these attitudes reflect individual personalities within the field rather than inherent characteristics of the field itself.

## The Homogeneous Grouping Controversy

Closely linked to the concern of elitist attitudes is the controversy over homogeneous grouping—the common practice of grouping high-ability students in special classrooms or activities. This controversy has resurfaced repeatedly in American schools. Rosenthal and Jacobson (1968) advanced the argument that grouping by ability lowered the expectations and consequently the achievement of students placed in lower-level classes. There is also the concern that removing gifted students from the regular classroom eliminates a positive academic role model for other students.

Criticism of ability grouping is usually leveled at the tracking of lower-achieving students, not at meeting the needs of high-ability students. Undoubtedly, steps should be taken to provide appropriate instructional strategies that enable all students to achieve their potential. However, denying appropriately challenging forms of enriched or accelerated curricula for able students is wholly indefensible.

Again, there is little evidence in the research literature to support any criticism of ability grouping. Kulik and Kulik (1984, 1987) conducted a careful review of the research designed to evaluate the effects of homogeneous grouping of secondary students based on ability. In each of their reports, the Kuliks concluded that ability grouping has minimal effects, either positive or negative, on the achievement of average or below-average students. Substantial evidence shows, however, that ability grouping has a positive effect on the achievement of gifted students. In a synthesis of research in gifted education, Feldhusen (1989) summarized substantial findings that address the concerns associated with ability grouping:

[grouping] . . . leads to higher academic achievement and better academic attitudes for the gifted and leads to no decline in achievement or attitude for the children who remain in the regular heterogeneous classroom. (p. 10)

In addition to this research evidence, pragmatic considerations support the concept of grouping highly able students. First, there is the obvious consideration of curricular structuring. When a student is capable of learning material in a fraction of the time required by his or her classmates, it is unreasonable to ask that student to fill the extra time with noncurricular activities. In a situation where accelerated learners are ignored, these students often become bored, frustrated, and resentful of their educational experience. In contrast, when high-ability students are placed in a fairly homogeneous classroom setting, they are more likely to share with intense interest and intellectual curiosity.

## Acceleration Versus Enrichment Controversy

The acceleration-enrichment debate has continued to be a critical focal point in gifted education. Unlike the case in the previous two controversies, this debate is most earnestly contended by researchers and practitioners within the field of gifted education. Those in favor of acceleration support learning experiences for the gifted that advance the pace of subject matter and are directed at the mastery and integration of content. Proponents of enrichment favor instructional strategies that emphasize student-directed exploration of subject matter, with emphasis on depth of analysis and integration of higher-order thinking skills. These models have been differentiated using the term *vertical* to refer to acceleration, suggesting a higher level, whereas *horizontal* has been used to describe the increased breadth of enrichment strategies.

The first issue to consider when dealing with the acceleration-enrichment controversy is that the line separating these two camps of thought is far from clear. Both approaches share common educational objectives. As Kirschenbaum (1984) concluded, ". . . enrichment offers advancement at an accelerated pace, and accelerated curricula provide students with enriching and broadening experiences in learning" (p. 96). For example, a ninth-grade gifted math class involving a unit on statistics would not only enrich the regular math curriculum but also challenge students to master advanced subject matter.

Davis and Rimm (1985) adopted operational definitions to distinguish between acceleration and enrichment. They defined acceleration to refer only to practices that result in advanced placement in grade level or course credit. Although enrichment may involve beyond-grade-level work, it does not result in the advanced academic standing of students. These definitions may be useful for administrative purposes, but this distinction gives no insight into the qualitative differences in the structure of these two instructional approaches.

Many specific strategies have been suggested as means of acceleration and enrichment. Most of the acceleration strategies listed here involve moving through existing coursework at a faster pace. Often this kind of acceleration can be accomplished simply by placing a student in a more advanced course. When this is possible, acceleration requires no special curriculum development or teaching loads and consequently is very cost-effective. Enrichment, in contrast, requires careful attention to curriculum development and skilled teaching to implement effectively.

In the course of the great debate concerning acceleration and enrichment, opponents of each view have made many heated claims. Julian Stanley (1978), a major advocate of acceleration, rigorously attacked enrichment as it is often practiced in the schools as ". . . a euphemism for busy work, fun and games, and whatever special subject matter the school wants to offer its many varieties of talent" (p. 3). Stanley is undoubtedly reacting to some of the many unfortunate stories told by his young students of extreme ability, but his criticism is directed at poor educational practices, not at enrichment per se. Enrichment programs that follow Renzulli's guidelines, which involve competent personnel and possess adequate resources, are likely to provide excellent educational opportunities to students who are moderately bright, creative, and task-committed.

Educators have several leading objections against the practice of acceleration. Many practitioners suggest that accelerated students are being "pushed" through the school and that the stress related to working with older, more mature students is detrimental to accelerated students' emotional development. Others fear that accelerated students will miss critical material if areas are skipped over, resulting in "learning gaps." However, extensive reviews of research on the effects of acceleration at both the elementary and secondary levels indicate that acceleration promotes achievement and show no indication that accelerated practices are detrimental to the social-emotional development of capable students (Daurio, 1979; Kulik & Kulik, 1984).

Despite these assurances, teachers and school administrators are often skeptical about the practice of acceleration. In a survey of coordinators of gifted programs, school psychologists, principals, and teachers, Southern, Jones, and Fiscus (1989) found that even professionals in gifted education maintained reservations about acceleration. These researchers found that fears of emotional stress caused by acceleration are of more concern than reservations about the accelerated students' ability to do higher-level work. This report concludes with a challenge to researchers studying the effects of acceleration to target their findings to practitioners.

Several efforts have been made to integrate the practices of enrichment and acceleration in a single model of gifted education. One example is the suggestion that acceleration and enrichment should not be seen simply as two opposing types of curricula for the gifted, but as two sets of learning styles and needs different groups of gifted learners exhibit (Colangelo & Zaffrann, 1979). In this conceptualization, enrichment programming is more suited for students with needs for self-directed exploration of subject matter whereas acceleration is more appropriate for students who are achievement-oriented. In another curricular model, Cox, Kelly, and Brinson (1988) suggested implementing enrichment curricula for a broad base of gifted students along with specific acceleration strategies for a subset of the gifted population.

## Implications for Counselors as Advocates

Inevitably, a counselor dedicated to the advocacy of appropriate educational experiences for gifted students will encounter situations related to these controversies and perhaps many others. Here are some examples of controversial situations in which a secondary school counselor might become involved:

Case 1. A highly talented eighth grader who masters first-year algebra and geometry during a special summer program requests to take second-year algebra in the high school. The teacher of this course expresses concern that the student will be too immature socially to function in the classroom.

Case 2. A student complains that the independent research project being conducted by students in the honors American history class is far more interesting than the traditional instruction that she experiences in her regular history class. This student did not have the minimum grade point average necessary for placement in the honors class.

Case 3. Reservations are expressed at a faculty meeting concerning the proposed implementation of advanced placement courses. An administrator complains that the time and resources required for the program would serve a group of students who are already advantaged and that more attention should be given to remedial courses for disadvantaged students.

In each of these situations the counselor has the opportunity to intervene as an advocate for gifted students. Working from the theoretical basis established at the beginning of this chapter, the counselor can build a substantial case for meeting the specific needs of individuals or groups of students. In each case, questions relating to the three principles underlying effective education for gifted students need to be asked:

1. Is the recommendation in question taking into account the developmental needs of the student or group of students?
2. How is the recommended practice actually different from the traditional curricular options available to students? Does the characteristic that differentiates the practice complement the differential needs of the student concerned?
3. Is the recommendation made in proactive response to the specific needs of the student in question or is it made in reaction to concerns of other individuals or school policies?

Applying these principles to the cases above, the counselor has the opportunity to advocate and defend an appropriate response. Here are some possible interventions the counselor/advocate might use in response to the three cases listed above:

Case 1. In the first case where the talented eighth grader masters the first-year algebra and geometry in a summer program and requests advancement, the counselor can be assured that substantial research indicates that young gifted students have performed very successfully, both academically and socially, in above-grade accelerated situations. The counselor should then seek evidence that the student in question demonstrates differential competence and the social maturity to support acceleration. Evidence of competence should be objective, possibly including documentation from the student's summer program of standardized achievement test scores. Teachers or the counselor should document in writing an evaluation of the student's social maturity. Finally, the counselor may need to address the logistical concerns of scheduling and transportation should the student need to move to a different building for math classes.

Case 2. In the second situation where a student wants the more stimulating honors curriculum, the school policy of setting a minimum grade point average for students to attend honors classes without exception might well be called for review. In a proactive sense, the counselor should concentrate on helping this student evaluate and define her own educational objectives and needs. Attempts to move this student into the honors section should be initiated only when and if the student herself decides that the honors curriculum meets her educational needs.

Case 3. In the last situation where reservations are expressed concerning implementation of advanced placement courses, the counselor might defend the expenditure of resources for talented students using the same egalitarian argument used to support remedial classes: the necessity of providing differential educational opportunities that meet specific needs of students. It would be essential in this case for proponents to have some objective assessment of the demand for advanced placement classes. However, care should be taken not to frame the controversy in a "one or the other" context. Rarely is the funding of gifted programs at the direct expense of remedial education. The issue at hand in this situation is providing appropriate education for all students, not promoting one population of students at the expense of another.

## Educating Gifted Students: Four Curricular Models

There has been a substantial increase in the development of alternative curricular designs for gifted secondary students in recent years. Responding to the growing awareness in American education of the special needs of high-ability students, researchers and practitioners across the country have committed their energies to the development of specialized curricula and programs. This effort has resulted in a diverse group of curricular models that are currently functioning in schools. These models vary widely in objectives, structure, content, and target populations. Some have originated from a need recognized in a specific population of gifted students; others have been developed in response to a broader spectrum of talents.

The diversity and number of curricular alternatives for gifted students are far too broad to review thoroughly in this chapter. Four prominent models have been chosen here for purposes of illustrating the diversity of practices currently used to meet the needs of gifted secondary students. Although each of these four models offers important contributions to the field, these examples are far from inclusive of all the many successful practices and curricular designs available to educators of the gifted and talented. Counselors who desire to investigate curricular options more fully should refer to some of the excellent books available on the topic, such as June Maker's book, *Teaching Models in Education of the Gifted* (1982).

In reviewing these four models, the counselor should keep in mind that most schools do not employ a single model or program to meet the needs of all gifted students. In an extensive national survey of American schools, Cox, Daniel, and Boston (1985) found that a large percentage of schools were using various methods to meet the needs of able learners. Unfortunately, many of these practices were found to be fragmented and discontinuous in scope and were unsatisfactory in meeting the full-time needs of gifted students. In response to this finding, one of the most important recommendations of this report centers on the need for educational programming for the gifted to originate from a single, cohesive philosophy of education for able learners.

Keeping this recommendation in mind, schools should not simply pick and choose from the practices suggested by these models. Instead, an integrative approach should be employed, basing all curricular options on a central conception of what constitutes appropriate education of gifted students. The Pyramid Model, described by Cox et al. (1985), shows how diverse curriculum approaches can be combined to create a strong districtwide program.

## SMPY and the Talent Search Model

In the late 1960s, a few young boys who were exceptionally talented in mathematical reasoning ability were brought to the attention of Julian Stanley, a professor of psychology at Johns Hopkins University. Dr. Stanley discovered that their local public schools were far from meeting the educational needs of these highly able learners. It was determined that many of these exceptional students were capable of doing mathematical coursework far beyond that expected in their grade level. Motivated by this discovery, Stanley initiated the Study of Mathematically Precocious Youth (SMPY) at Johns Hopkins in 1971. The goal of this program was to identify young students of extraordinary mathematical reasoning ability and to help them find appropriate curricular alternatives to develop their abilities.

In order to identify these highly able students, the concept of an annual talent search was initiated in 1972. Stanley, an internationally recognized psychometrician, found that traditional mathematical achievement tests used in the middle or junior high schools were far too "low ended" to differentiate among students of exceptional ability effectively. Stanley found that students who scored in the 99th percentile on such tests included individuals who still represented a broad range of abilities (Benbow, 1986). Stanley chose the College Board's Scholastic Aptitude Test math component (SAT-M) as an alternative test to identify young, precocious mathematics students. This test, designed to measure mathematical reasoning ability in 12th-grade students, was found to be a reliable and practical means of discriminating among these young, capable learners.

The Talent Search Model grew through the 1970s to include the identification and advisement of nearly 10,000 students. In the 1980s, the Talent Search Model was expanded to a national perspective and was administered through a series of national and local talent searches conducted through various higher education institutes throughout the country. Although each of these talent searches keeps to the same basic program of using "out-of-level testing" as a means of identifying highly gifted students, precise identification criteria and educational options made available to identified students vary from location to location. Recent developments in the Talent Search Model include the use of a verbal score on the SAT (SAT-V) as a means of identifying students with precocious verbal abilities and the use of the American College Testing Assessment Program as a means of identification.

Most talent searches are open to students in the seventh or eighth grades who achieve high test scores on standardized achievement tests designed for their grade level (identification cutoffs range from the 95th to the 97th percentile on these tests). Students who meet these cutoffs and learn of the talent search through school publications or a counselor sign up independently to take one of the standardized aptitude tests offered on a national basis several times each year. Students request that these test scores be reported directly to a talent search institution. Students who achieve a test score that meets the criteria of that particular talent search are then invited to participate in several advanced educational opportunities.

Counselors are urged to contact one of the national talent search offices for exact information on qualification and registration procedures. A list of these offices is included in the Resources section at the end of this book.

Evolving from the SMPY and Talent Search models are several promising practices that the school counselor can use (Stanley & Benbow, 1982). These practices include the Diagnostic Testing followed by Prescriptive Instruction (DP-TI) model. Using this model, high-ability students are given a standardized test, which is then analyzed to identify specific content areas of lower competence that require instruction. Students are then assigned to a teaching strategy that specifically addresses the area in which work is needed. Another important contribution of the SMPY model is the identification and recommendation of several educational options for students identified by the talent search process. Most of these alternatives are accelerated in nature and many will be discussed more fully in the next section of this chapter.

Although the growth and success of the Talent Search Model have been widely evident in the last two decades and substantial documentation of the efficacy of recommended practices exists (e.g., Brody & Benbow, 1987), the Talent Search Model has not escaped criticism. Because the talent searches involve rigorous entry standards and heavily recommend acceleration strategies, the most common complaints against talent searches follow the same lines as do arguments about elitism and acceleration in general. More specific concerns have been raised concerning the fact that the use of ACT and SAT scores may hinder the identification of gifted women and minorities. In a defense of the Talent Search Model, Van Tassel-Baska (1984) argued that the use of out-of-level testing has increased, rather than reduced, the number of students identified as gifted. In addition, the Talent Search Model has been used successfully for the specific purpose of identifying talent in young women and minority students.

In regard to the educational philosophy set out in the beginning of this chapter, the SMPY and Talent Search models fulfill most of the criteria for a successful program for the gifted. To begin with, the Talent Search Model focuses on meeting the needs that, by definition, differentiate this group of students from their peers. Along with considering the developmental needs of gifted learners, the Talent Search and SMPY models recommend accelerated strategies that carefully match curricular development to the students' level of competence within specific subject areas. The SMPY and Talent Search models also make allowances for different levels of ability among students who are identified. These models emphasize curricular flexibility and alternative educational opportunities to meet individual student needs.

One of the strongest attributes of the SMPY model is the proactive role of "educational counselors" as suggested by Benbow (1986, p. 23). Benbow advocated the role of educational coordinators of the gifted rather than teachers of the gifted. This role emphasizes the assessment of individual students' educational needs and the placement of students in appropriate learning environments rather than emphasizing the development of a separate curriculum for gifted learners. The flexibility and individualization this role affords suggests an appropriate model for the counselor who might not be directly involved in the curricular design issues in the gifted classroom. This role is also optimal for counselors who work with students in schools with little or no resources for gifted students.

It is the narrow focus of the SMPY/Talent Search Model that poses the greatest possibility of limitation when evaluated in reference to our proposed philosophical basis of gifted education. The degree of this limitation depends on one's working definition of giftedness. Identification of gifted students solely by standardized testing that uses an arbitrary numerical cutoff limits this model's flexibility to respond to the differential definitions of gifted populations. Any population of gifted students who for one reason or another do not do well on achievement or aptitude tests of mathematical or verbal reasoning would be overlooked by this model. In addition, any model that focuses on acceleration to the exclusion of enrichment, particularly in subject areas other than math, may not meet the holistic needs of gifted learners.

## The Purdue Secondary Model

The Purdue Secondary Model for Gifted and Talented Youth was developed by John Feldhusen and his colleagues at Purdue University and is based on their years of research and service to gifted youth (Feldhusen, 1980). The model is intended to meet both the cognitive and affective needs of gifted students through a comprehensive program of counseling and differential educational opportunities.

As in the case of all appropriate models of gifted education, the Purdue Secondary Model begins with an appropriate rationale for the differential education of the gifted. The model builds on Feldhusen's (1980) conception of giftedness, which includes (a) general intellectual ability, (b) positive self-concept, (c) achievement motivation, and (d) talent. Feldhusen builds the case that students who demonstrate these characteristics need special educational programming to develop their potential. Appropriate educational opportunities include a variety of strategies, including broad-based intellectual challenges in both accelerated and enriched curricula.

The structure of the Purdue model includes three major areas of differentiated programming for gifted secondary students that are categorized in 11 conceptual "blocks." The first area of emphasis is in providing appropriate counseling services. The Purdue model recognizes the vital role school counselors play in secondary programs. The identification of differential abilities leads to the need to identify appropriate educational options for particular types of talent. In addition, the secondary school counselor fills a vital role in the personal and vocational counseling of gifted students.

The second major component of the Purdue model is the seminar. The seminar consists of a separate class for gifted students that emphasizes student-directed research, writing, presentations, and open discussions. The Purdue model stresses the need for the seminar to be taught by an outstanding teacher who can also fill the role of mentor for exceptionally able students. There is no limit to the precise topic of the seminar, rather a challenge to make the scope of the seminar relevant to the educational needs of students and contain sufficient flexibility for students to pursue individual interests within the topic area.

The third general area of the Purdue Secondary Model includes a wide variety of curriculum opportunities (blocks 3 through 11) that are intended to provide the model with the breadth and flexibility necessary to meet the holistic needs of gifted populations. Some of these options, such as advanced placement courses and math-science acceleration (blocks 3 and 5), include acceleration strategies suggested by the SMPY/Talent Search models. However, the Purdue model adds a far more comprehensive list of alternatives than that suggested by the SMPY model. Provisions for foreign language development, exploration of the arts, and vocational education opportunities round out the suggested educational alternatives.

An important characteristic of the Purdue model is the diversity of resources and methods it includes in meeting the needs of able learners. Special workshops and seminars are suggested throughout the model as successful means of addressing particular developmental concerns of gifted students, such as vocational development or college planning. Special Saturday morning programs or classes are also suggested as a means of addressing the needs of various gifted populations (Feldhusen & Robinson-Wyman, 1980). In order to integrate various academic disciplines in a suggested curriculum, the Purdue model suggests a team teaching approach to developing curricular units. Finally, the Purdue model incorporates the use of mentoring, both as a model for instruction and for vocational development for gifted students.

Returning again to the theoretical foundation as a basis of evaluation, the Purdue model more than adequately addresses each of the three conceptual areas. First, the Purdue model has been systematically adapted to meet the developmental needs of gifted learners as they progress through school. Second, the synthesis of acceleration and enrichment alternatives, in combination with the broad scope of topical areas included by the model, suggests the flexibility necessary to address the specific needs of various populations of the gifted. This synthesis represents the strength of the eclectic approach to curriculum development (Feldhusen, 1984). Third, when implemented in a comprehensive fashion, the Purdue model functions in a proactive mode, with curricular options functioning to meet the needs of gifted learners as these needs become apparent.

The potential strength of the Purdue model does not come without cost, however. The major limitation of the model is its complexity and need for trained staff to implement the program successfully. The Purdue model suggests ways in which curricula for the gifted should be structured and what needs should be addressed. The model does not include the exact curriculum or the pragmatic details of implementing such a system. Instead, the model assumes that a given school will have the trained personnel, resources, and administrative support to implement such a program.

There is no doubt that to implement the Purdue model at a local school level will require substantial expertise in the areas of curricular development, counseling, program coordination, and mentoring activities. A comprehensive program will also require considerable support from school administration, teachers, and the community. If these requirements seem too intimidating for the small, rural, or poorly funded school, programming might be limited to various components of the model such as the Saturday morning activities. Feldhusen also suggests that cooperative arrangements might be used where services and programs are shared by several schools.

## The Enrichment Triad/Revolving Door Identification Model

The Enrichment Triad/Revolving Door Identification Model (Renzulli et al., 1981) is the most widely used system of identification and curriculum modification in the United States today. The Enrichment Triad Model includes three types of enrichment activities for students. These include:

## General Exploratory Activities

These activities, called Type I activities, are experiences designed to help learners to understand their areas of personal interests. Type I experiences are broad exploratory experiences in which students are exposed to a wide variety of content areas and topics.

## Group Training Activities

These activities, called Type II activities, consist of materials, methods, and instructional techniques that enhance high-level thinking skills and facilitate feeling processes. These activities might include critical thinking skills programs, problem-solving training, reflective thinking, training in inquiry, training in creative problem solving, awareness development, and other creative or productive thinking activities.

## Individual or Small Group Investigations

These Type III activities provide students with opportunities to investigate a real problem by using appropriate inquiry methods. Students engaging in Type III activities must have strong interests and task commitment. In these activities, students use the techniques of practicing professionals in a wide variety of fields. Type III activities are special projects that require a great deal of autonomy and initiative on the part of the students as well as skilled mentoring on the part of the resource teacher who serves as their assistant in the process.

The Revolving Door Identification Model is paired with the Enrichment Triad Model. This is the process by which a pool of approximately 15% to 20% of the student population is selected. Generally, these are students with above-average intelligence as measured by a variety of intelligence instruments; who have also shown evidence of ability to commit themselves to tasks; and who have above-average creativity. These students are exposed to Type I activities and receive Type II process training usually on a weekly basis. During the time the students are exposed to Type I enrichment activities and Type II training, it is assumed that they will become interested in the more challenging Type III activities. Students "revolve into" these options as they show an interest and a desire to pursue advanced work.

Generally, an Enrichment Triad/Revolving Door Identification Model gifted program is implemented through a pull-out process. That is, students are pulled out of the regular classroom for a period of 1 to 3 hours a week in which they engage in special activities. Usually these activities take place in a resource room with a resource teacher specially trained in facilitating the students in the three types of activities. In order for these programs to be successful, Reis and Renzulli (1984) contended that they must hold certain key features. The first, which they call "the golden rule," is that the more thoroughly teachers, students, parents, and administrators understand the structure of the model, the easier it is to implement the identification procedure and the learning activity. Therefore orientation, materials, and in-service training are all used to help teachers, parents, and administrators to be aware of the structure of the program. It is particularly important that all populations involved understand the language of the model. The second key feature of successful triad revolving door models is planning prior to program implementation. Reis and Renzulli suggested that in each district a planning team be established to make decisions about how the model will be tailored to accommodate the unique characteristics and resources of the participating schools. They recommended that the planning team consist of volunteers and persons selected by the administrators, and that people such as teachers, school psychologists, media specialists, parents, principals, and central office administrators be on the team. The planning team decides which grade levels are to be included, the size of the talent pool, and the criteria to be used in choosing the talent pool.

Key feature three involves in-service and administrative support. Reis and Renzulli (1984) claimed that for any new program to be successful, in-service training must be provided for all persons who will be involved. They stressed the importance of school administrators in this process. The three kinds of in-service recommended are formal in-service (short sessions focusing on specific topics and skills), informal in-service (regular interaction of teachers of the gifted with other staff members), and finally, distribution of materials that describe the procedures being used in the gifted program.

Key feature four, the schoolwide enrichment team, is a group made up of the principal, the resource teacher, three or four classroom teachers, some parents, and sometimes a student. These teams put into practice an essential part of the philosophy of the Triad Revolving Door model—that the total educational experience of all students should include varying amounts and levels of enrichment. The team plans and acts as a clearinghouse for visiting speakers, field trips, artistic performances, and other activities that will involve the entire school as well as those students identified as gifted. The team evaluates enrichment materials and decides which ones fit with the regular curriculum. The team recruits faculty members and community resource persons who can help with the enrichment sessions. It also reviews what is happening on television, summer programs, fairs, and contests that is related to academic and other opportunities for student participation in hobbies, theater, and local groups.

Key feature five, program ownership, means that everybody should feel as if the gifted program is their own, and that the total range of services provided are available to those who need and want them. Reis and Renzulli (1984) recommended that the resource room and appropriate activities, games, and materials be used for all children. These materials can be circulated from classroom to classroom. Enrichment experiences can be shared with other teachers and students whenever possible and, finally, the results of students' Type III activity can be shared with other students.

Key feature six, student orientation, holds that talent pool students should be given a detailed orientation about what services and opportunities are available so that they can avail themselves of these opportunities intelligently. The students must not only know what all the activities will entail but how the activities will be evaluated.

Key feature seven, communication with prime interest groups, means that even the general public will be kept aware of what is happening in the gifted education program. Newsletters, invitations to visit the resource room, and opportunities to view completed Type III products are all ways of communicating with the public as well as with the interest groups of parents, others teachers, and other students.

Key feature eight is flexibility. Reis and Renzulli (1984) suggested that the flexibility of resource teachers is one of the most important characteristics of this model. Teachers must be flexible so that programs can be tailored to particular students and to particular schools.

Key feature nine is evaluation and program monitoring. Reis and Renzulli (1984) claimed that programs cannot exist without a schoolwide commitment to evaluation and monitoring. Evaluation not only provides important data for research but also helps to refine and further develop the program. Renzulli and his colleagues (1981) developed a wide variety of evaluation instruments that can be used to measure the outcomes of this model.

If these key features of successful enrichment programs are put into place, does this ensure that this model will meet the needs of all gifted students? The advantages of the Enrichment Triad/Revolving Door Identification Model are that these programs do allow at least some interaction with intellectual peers; that only a small number of teachers are needed; that the teacher can concentrate on thinking and research skills because of having no responsibility for basic skills; and that when the gifted child is out of the regular classroom, others can rise to the attention of the teacher. According to Belcastro (1987), there are still clear disadvantages for at least some gifted students. Belcastro claims that pull-out programs that are tied to the regular curriculum are quite rare. Instead he says that many such programs are a smorgasbord of offerings that have no common thread and that are disconnected from the regular curriculum. Too often this becomes a collection of games and activities that does not actually constitute a qualitatively different curriculum for the gifted. For example, the problem-solving strategies that are taught may not be associated with such content areas as biology or mathematics but instead with puzzles or mysteries. Creativity is used in future problem solving rather than applied to mathematics or social studies. In addition, the inclusion of so many above-average students with very gifted students often results in a dilution of the program so that it is not truly a differentiated program.

According to Belcastro (1987), a program that meets for only a few hours a week has a minimal impact on the academic experience of the gifted student. Time out for the gifted program is often time misused. In addition, students who miss regular classes in order to go to the resource room are often made to finish the work they missed at other times, thus putting more pressure on them. Because of the short amount of time, students gain few opportunities to interact with their intellectual peers. Faster pacing is seldom used, although the model allows for it. Even though a wide variety of strategies is encouraged, in practice this often does not occur.

Perhaps Belcastro's (1987) most serious criticism of pull-out programs is this: Although the Enrichment Triad Model is simple and expedient, it creates the impression that something substantial is being done for the intellectually gifted. The pull-out program, he says, not only delays but actually impedes progress toward sounder programs because it allows administrators and teachers to be comfortable with the status quo.

Cox and Daniel (1983) also listed disadvantages. They found that regular teachers resented the program because gifted students found the classes more exciting or stimulating than their own; that project planning was difficult when a week intervened between classes; that programs tended to be isolated, fragmented, time-limited, and lacking in continuity with other school programs; that one staff person could not be sufficiently skilled to do the program justice; that occasionally negative attitudes toward gifted students in regular classroom were instilled; and that teachers saw the pull-out program as an interruption of their regular programs, inducing hostility toward gifted programs in general.

Therefore, a major paradox exists in gifted education today. The most widely practiced model is increasingly becoming the target of criticism from researchers, scholars, and theorists as well as from parents of gifted students.

## Autonomous Learner Model

The Autonomous Learner Model was developed by George Betts (1981) as a secondary model of gifted education. The program was developed not only for academically talented students but also for students talented in creative thinking, leadership, and visual and performing arts. This program brings all these students together for a series of activities designed to create "autonomous learners"—that is—students who are able to identify their own learning experiences and to implement their own learning projects. Gifted students are given the flexibility of determining intensive courses of study and units of learning for themselves. The Autonomous Learner Model is organized as a class that meets 1 hour a day 5 days a week. It can last for as long as 6 years.

Students are identified by a wide variety of procedures including tests of intellectual ability, creativity, leadership, and measures of a variety of talents. Most of the program is oriented toward developing the basic skills necessary for autonomous learning, for increasing self-understanding or self-acceptance, for increasing understanding and acceptance of giftedness, for developing effective interpersonal relationships, and for helping students to become more positive and productive individuals. The Autonomous Learner Model consists of five components: (1) orientation, (2) individual development, (3) enrichment activities, (4) seminars, and (5) in-depth study.

## Orientation

In this component of the Autonomous Learner Model students are oriented toward the program in general and are encouraged to learn about themselves. During orientation to the program students learn to understand their own giftedness through readings and activities about gifted individuals. Group building activities involve team building and new games in order to facilitate group cohesiveness. A self-understanding program starts each student on the way to understanding his or her own needs, interests, and values. And finally, an overview of the opportunities and responsibilities available through the program is given.

## Individual Development

Individual development involves skills and awarenesses for the individual's personal growth. This component may include learning skills such as study skills and learning strategies; personal understanding exercises; interpersonal skills training; and career education and development.

## Enrichment Activities

Enrichment activities are closely tied to academic development. These activities involve exploring topics of interest to the students. In addition, cultural activities and adventure trips provide insights into ideas and experiences beyond those usually encountered in the classroom. Students may engage in service activities and cross-age tutoring. Finally, biographical research is an important aspect of the enrichment activities offered through this model.

## Seminars

Seminars are the basic means by which students share the knowledge they have gained through this gifted education program. Seminars not only serve the purpose of sharing knowledge but also that of broadening the interests of students in the group. They are a way of providing peer teaching opportunities as well as a chance to work with community resource people to learn more about a topic of interest.

## In-Depth Study

In-depth study is a component that teaches the basic skills of intensive research and preparation of presentations. Students choose individual projects on a particular topic for in-depth study, and they also participate in group projects in which the group cooperates in exploring an interest. Mentorships are an important aspect of this component; students are linked with community resource individuals and other teachers in order to learn about these persons' areas of expertise. As a part of the in-depth study component students learn the skills necessary to make presentations about their individual projects. In addition, they learn evaluation methods to enable them to assess their own work and that of others in their group.

The Autonomous Learner Model has become increasingly popular in secondary schools in this country. However, although it is the result of 5 years of research, planning, and experimentation, it has not generated a great deal of outcome research or comparative research. Therefore, little is known about how this model compares to others in terms of students' growth. It is important to recognize that this model is so highly psychological in nature that outcomes should be measured not just in terms of academic achievement, but also in terms of personal growth.

## The Counselor and the Curriculum

It should be apparent from the foregoing discussion that each of these curriculum models may be associated with a unique set of student needs and concerns. Each model essentially shapes a very different kind of gifted student with his or her own perception of what it means to be gifted. In addition, each model may be associated with particular presenting problems for counselors' clients.

The acceleration model is likely to produce students in high school who have advanced far ahead of their peers in at least one area. These students may already have exhausted all the resources available to them in their area of talent in their high school. For instance, the student who has been radically accelerated in math may already have completed calculus after a few summers at summer institutes at Johns Hopkins or Duke or a similar university program. This leaves the counselor with the job of determining in what way those math courses will be counted toward the student's graduation requirements and which courses in other areas should be substituted for that student's math courses. Another related difficulty may be that the student who has experienced highly accelerated, intellectually stimulating classes during the summer may return during the regular school year only to feel bored and frustrated with the slow pace of high school classes. Counselors may need to help students deal with these frustrations by assisting them to discover other sources of intellectual stimulation as well as ways of making the materials they are studying more interesting to them.

One other outcome of accelerated programs is that students, for the first time, may have spent long periods of time with their intellectual peers. As a result, they have often made close friendships and have discovered a social group that has more importance for them than any they have experienced before. As a result, the return from a summer program or the return to a regular program from a highly accelerated program of any kind may be associated with feelings of loneliness and alienation.

As mentioned before, for some students accelerated programs do lead to feelings of internal pressure and stress. It is not likely that the programs themselves are the cause, but rather the interaction of the fast-paced program with the student's perfectionism. Nevertheless, counselors need to help students adjust their personal expectations to the kind of competition they encounter in these classes.

It is difficult to pinpoint what kind of counseling difficulties may be associated with Feldhusen's model of gifted education. It has already been noted that Feldhusen's Purdue Secondary model has a strong counseling component. Because programs are closely tailored to students' needs, it is likely that fewer psychological problems result from a mismatch of curriculum and student needs. Perhaps the only possible negative outcome of the Feldhusen model of gifted education is that students may become overreliant on individualized programming and the use of the counselor's time. It is also possible that some healthy, self-actualizing students may find counseling activities oriented toward building self-esteem to be superfluous.

The Renzulli Enrichment Triad/Revolving Door Identification Model may lead to a few characteristic counseling problems. The first arises when highly gifted students are not admitted to the gifted education program. Because Renzulli's identification procedures involve selecting students of above-average intelligence who are task-committed and who demonstrate creativity, it is often possible that a very high-IQ student will not be admitted. Most frequently, the very high-IQ student who is not admitted to an enrichment program is an underachiever whom teachers have a difficult time motivating. Occasionally, however, teachers or program directors have vented their resentment or hostility toward very bright students by denying them access to the program based on a subjective judgment that the student is "test-bright but not creative." The unhappy scenario that often unfolds in this case is one in which the student and parent appeal their case to an administrator or board. The gifted student then is admitted to the gifted program only to learn that there is little there to meet his or her needs. Extremely bright students may feel that enrichment programs are too insubstantial and slow-paced for their intellectual needs. Students in these situations may seek the counselor's aid in finding more challenging activities or even in making the enrichment program more rigorous.

Another counseling problem that may be associated with the enrichment model may occur when students object to psychological exercises used in Type II activities. Many Type II activities are structured group experiences that were originally designed for encounter groups or training groups led by psychologists. Feedback and self-disclosure activities performed as part of communications skills training may be perceived as overly threatening and intense. Values clarification exercises may anger those students who have been brought up within traditional homes where absolute values are taught. Finally, fantasy exercises may be disturbing to students whose thought processes are already somewhat "loose" or unstructured.

Problems that may result from Betts's Autonomous Learner Model may be similar to those that result from Type II enrichment activities. Because Betts's model is the most psychologically oriented of all the models, students who are desirous of academic content rather than process activities may be particularly dissatisfied. Self-exploration and self-reflection may strike cynical, verbally brilliant students as silly or irrelevant. Gifted individualists who do not wish to share their feelings with other students may reject group activities. Counselors should ensure that all psychological activities such as fantasies, self-disclosure and feedback exercises, encounter techniques, and awareness techniques are used appropriately.

This means that these activities should be developed under the supervision of a counselor, counseling psychologist, or school psychologist to ensure that they are appropriate to students' developmental levels and that they do not involve exercises that are too intimate or too threatening.

Also, all ethical constraints about which counselors and psychologists are aware should be observed with these activities. Participants should be allowed confidentiality, and all activities should be voluntary. Students who wish to drop out of these activities at any point should be able to do so without negative evaluations.

With appropriate safeguards, Type II enrichment activities, and many components of Betts's model, can be helpful to gifted students. As part of the curriculum, they may also serve as sources of primary prevention of psychological adjustment problems. Students who are experiencing depression, loneliness, or stress, or those who are having difficulty with their academic program may come to the attention of the teacher or facilitator of these programs, who may then refer the students for counseling in a timely fashion.

It is clear from the preceding discussion that counselors should work closely with teachers of the gifted in developing curriculum. By helping teachers to develop gifted programs that are developmentally appropriate, carefully differentiated, and proactive, counselors can ensure that gifted education programs will fit the students' needs and create lasting contributions to the school curriculum.

The Council for Exceptional Children—the Association for the Gifted, has developed standards for programs involving gifted and talented students (CEC, 1989). Program design is the plan by which instruction is delivered to gifted and talented students. According to CEC-TAG, gifted and talented programs should be a flexible system of viable program options throughout the general and special education structures that are compatible with and matched to the strengths, needs, and interests of gifted and talented students. The Resources section at the end of this book includes general guidelines for program design that counselors may wish to share with teachers of the gifted and facilitators of gifted programs.

## Summary

Academic guidance programs for gifted students should be developmental in that they should take into account progressive changes known to occur among gifted learners; they should be differential, based on quantitative as well as qualitative differences; and they should be proactive. Counselors need to be aware of the various controversies surrounding gifted education, such as concerns about elitism, grouping, and acceleration versus enrichment, in order to be effective advocates for gifted students. Finally, counselors need to understand the impact of major curricular models on gifted students' adjustment and psychological growth.

## References

Belcastro, F. (1987). Elementary pull-out program—boon or bane? *Roeper Review*, *9*(4), 208–212.

Benbow, C. P. (1986). SMPY's model for teaching mathematically precocious students. In J. S. Renzulli (Ed.), *Systems and models in programs for the gifted and talented* (pp. 1–25). Mansfield Center, CT: Creative Learning.

Betts, G. T. (1981). Autonomous learning and the gifted: A secondary model. In I. Sato (Ed.), *Secondary programs for the gifted/talented*. Ventura, CA: Ventura County Superintendent of Schools Office.

Brody, L. E., & Benbow, C. P. (1987). Accelerative strategies: How effective are they for the gifted? *Gifted Child Quarterly*, *31*, 105–110.

Buescher, T. (1987). Counseling gifted adolescents: A curriculum model for students, parents, and professionals. *Gifted Child Quarterly*, *31*(2), 90–93.

Colangelo, N., & Brower, P. (1987). Labeling gifted youngsters: Long-term impact on families. *Gifted Child Quarterly*, *31*(2), 75–78.

Colangelo, N., & Zaffrann, R. T. (1979). *New voices in counseling the gifted*. Dubuque, IA: Kendall/Hunt.

Council for Exceptional Children-The Association for the Gifted (TAG). (1989). *Standards for programs involving gifted and talented*. Reston, VA: ERIC Clearinghouse on Handicapped and Gifted Children.

Cox, J., & Daniel, N. (1983). Specialized schools for high ability students. *G/C/T*, *28*, 2–9.

Cox, J., Daniel, N., & Boston, B. (1985). *Educating able learners: Programs and promising practices*. Austin: University of Texas Press.

Cox, J. R., Kelly, J., & Brison, P. (1988). The Pyramid Project: Implementing the Richardson study recommendations. *Roeper Review*, *11*(1), 20–28.

Daurio, S. P. (1979). Educational enrichment versus acceleration: A review of the literature. In W. C. George, S. J. Cohn, & J. C. Stanley (Eds.), *Educating the gifted, acceleration and enrichment* (pp. 13–63). Baltimore: Johns Hopkins University Press.

Davis, G. A., & Rimm, S. B. (1985). *Education of the gifted and talented.* Englewood Cliffs, NJ: Prentice-Hall.

Delisle, J. R. (1984). *Gifted kids speak out.* New York: Walker.

Feldhusen, J. F. (Ed.). (1980). *Concept curriculum for the gifted.* Matteson, IL: Region I South Area Service Center for the Gifted.

Feldhusen, J. F. (1984). Myth: Gifted education means having a program! Meeting the needs of gifted students through differential programming. *Gifted Child Quarterly, 26*(1), 37–41.

Feldhusen, J. F. (1989, March). Synthesis of research on gifted youth. *Educational Leadership, 9*(1), 6–11.

Feldhusen, J. F., & Robinson-Wyman, A. R. (1980). Super Saturday: Design and implementation of Purdue's special program for gifted children. *Gifted Child Quarterly, 24*, 15–21.

Gardner, H. (1983). *Frames of mind.* New York: Basic Books.

Kirschenbaum, R. J. (1984). Perspectives on programming models: Acceleration and enrichment. *Roeper Review, 7*(2), 95–98.

Kulik, J. A., & Kulik, C. L. C. (1984). Effects of accelerated instruction on students. *Review of Educational Research, 54*(3), 409–425.

Kulik, J. A., & Kulik, C. C. (1987). Effects of ability grouping on student achievement. *Equity and Excellence, 23*(2), 22–30.

Maker, C. J. (1982). *Teaching models in education of the gifted.* Rockville, MD: Aspen.

Myers, D. G., & Ridl, J. (1981, February-March). Aren't all children gifted? *Today's Education, General Edition, 30*GS–33GS.

Reis, S. M., & Renzulli, J. S. (1984). Key features of successful programs for the gifted and talented. *Educational Leadership, 4*(7), 28–34.

Renzulli, J. S., Reis, S. M., & Smith, L. H. (1981). *The Revolving Door Identification Model.* Mansfield Center, CT: Creative Learning Press.

Rosenthal, R. J., & Jacobson, L. (1968). *Pygmalion in the classroom; Teacher expectations and pupils' intellectual development.* New York: Holt, Rinehart & Winston.

Southern, W. T., Jones, E. D., & Fiscus, E. D. (1989). Practitioner objections to the academic acceleration of gifted chidlren. *Gifted Child Quarterly, 33*(1), 29–35.

Stanley, J. C. (1978). Educational non-acceleration: An instructional tragedy. *Gifted Child Quarterly, 1*(3), 2–5.

Stanley, J. C., & Benbow, C. P. (1982). Educating mathematically precocious youth: Twelve policy recommendations. *Educational Researcher, 11*(5), 4–9.

Stanley, J. C., & Benbow, C. P. (1983). Extremely young college grads: Evidence of their success. *College and University, 58*(4), 361–371.

Sternberg, R. J., & Davidson, J. E. (1986). *Conceptions of giftedness*. New York: Cambridge University Press.
Van Tassel-Baska, J. (1984). The talent search as an identification model. *Gifted Child Quarterly, 28*(4), 172–175.
Ward, V. S. (1985). Giftedness and personal development theoretical considerations. *Roeper Review, 8*(1), 6–10.

# Counseling the Underachieving Gifted Student

When a child's academic performance is much lower than would have been predicted by achievement test scores, IQ, or past academic performance, teachers and parents often turn to the counselor for an explanation. Why are the grades so low? Why won't the student participate in class? Underachieving gifted students have been a source of much controversy for educational researchers and many practical difficulties for the counselor and classroom teacher.

Educational researchers are in conflict about whether underachievement actually exists. Anastasi (1976) contended that underachievement is not even a legitimate category of academic behavior; the label is often based on comparisons of intelligence tests to achievement tests, which is inappropriate. Anastasi sees most underachievement as simply test error: A statistical artifact of imperfect methods of measurement.

Other authors (Dowdall & Colangelo, 1982; Whitmore, 1980) are concerned that there are too many definitions of the underachieving gifted. Dowdall and Colangelo found three different categories of definitions in their review of the literature: the difference between two standardized measures; the difference between a standardized measure and performance on some nonstandardized measures; and the difference between two nonstandardized measures. Within these categories there were scores of definitions. They concluded that "the variability of definitions is of a magnitude that makes the concept of underachieving gifted almost meaningless" (p. 179).

Nevertheless, many educators, at least at the elementary and secondary levels of schooling, have continued to attempt to identify the underachieving gifted, to draw conclusions about their behavior, and to develop remedial interventions (Bricklin & Bricklin, 1967; Fine & Pitts, 1980; Rimm, 1988; Whitmore, 1980).

## Common Issues for Underachievers

Despite the wide variability in definitions, commonalities do emerge among observations and measures of students who are not performing as expected. Dowdall and Colangelo (1982) found that across studies, the characteristics of gifted underachievers were much more similar to underachievers in general than to gifted students in general. In fact, they resemble gifted students only in their high scores on IQ tests, achievement tests, or earlier grades. Compared to achievers, gifted underachievers seem to be more socially immature (Hecht, 1975); have more emotional problems (Pringle, 1970); engage in more antisocial behavior (Bricklin & Bricklin, 1967); and have lower self-concepts (Colangelo & Pfleger, 1979; Whitmore, 1980).

## Social Immaturity

Gifted underachievers may be less well adjusted socially than gifted students in general. Their social immaturity is expressed in many ways. They may have difficulty making friends and they may not be able to sustain friendships. Gifted underachievers may have difficulty cooperating in a group, participating too much or not participating enough. They may dominate the group, or be too unassertive. They may show off, or engage in other behaviors that block the group's progress. Gifted underachievers in elementary years may have problems with separating from their parents during school hours. They may be overly dependent on teachers, or behave inappropriately toward adults. In games and sports, underachieving gifted students may be poor sports, finding it difficult to play by the rules and accept loss and failure in competition.

## Emotional Problems

Underachieving gifted children's emotional problems range from crying too easily to getting angry too easily. These children tend to be oversensitive or overly aggressive. On personality tests gifted underachievers show a wide variety of personalities but also some common emotional problems such as depression or anger. Personal problems may also be manifested as extreme lability, that is, changing from one mood to another very easily. The emotional problems of gifted underachievers tend to be long-term rather than situational.

## Antisocial Behavior

One of the most common findings about gifted underachievers is their tendency toward antisocial characteristics and behavior. In fact, on most personality tests, gifted underachievers look similar to sociopathic individuals. Sociopathic people have poorly developed consciences; are impulsive in their behavior; act out their anger by being aggressive toward people or destroying things; and tend to use their intelligence to deceive and "con" others.

Gifted students who engage in antisocial behavior may be those who are caught cheating on tests or stealing school property. They may hurt other children or take or destroy other children's toys. As adolescents, antisocial underachieving gifted students may engage in illegal activities such as selling drugs, shoplifting, or creating computer "viruses." Nevertheless, gifted underachievers' personalities are not entirely sociopathic or antisocial. A recent study by Arcenaux (1990) shows that although underachieving gifted students do possess such antisocial personality characteristics as impulsivity, need for play, and a self-centered orientation, these characteristics are paradoxically combined with a need for understanding and knowledge. Although they engage in behaviors that are not socially approved of, gifted underachievers seem to have a longing to understand their own behavior and the world around them. In contrast to the unthinking and unfeeling sociopath, the gifted underachiever may have the need for profound thought and for expressing intense feelings.

## Low Self-Concept

The majority of studies of gifted underachievers have also found that most students classified in this way have very low self-concepts. They are negative about themselves in many ways. They see themselves as unattractive, unlovable, and unintelligent. Despite high intelligence test scores or achievement test scores, many gifted underachievers are convinced of their own inability to succeed. Many feel that they do not deserve to succeed. Low self-esteem always has many causes. One of the major causes of gifted underachievers' low self-esteem, however, may be their persistently low grades. For gifted underachievers, negative academic feedback is a vicious cycle. Poor grades lead to low expectations of self, which lead to even lower performance. Many gifted underachievers do not see a way out of this vicious cycle.

It is likely that there is a "true" group of gifted underachievers, one that is not made up of people who simply represent measurement error. This chapter will examine the various kinds of underachievement, explore the causes of that behavior, and suggest ways in which counselors can redirect the academic behavior of this population.

## Varieties of Underachievement

Probably the most disturbing pattern of underachieving behavior is that in which a student's classroom performance does not match that student's scores on IQ tests, achievement tests, or other aptitude tests. It is important to explore the possible meanings of these discrepancies and to describe behaviors associated with each of these types of underachievement.

## Discrepancies Between IQ Score and Classroom Performance

Observed discrepancies between intelligence test scores and academic performance are perhaps the most common instances of underachievement. What are the possible explanations for this discrepancy? The following is a listing of some explanations for this form of underachievement.

## Hypothesis 1: *The Test Is Wrong*

In many cases, when a single high IQ score conflicts with all other measures, and when classroom behavior is consistently average or below average, the intelligence test score may simply be wrong. There is, after all, a margin of error for every intelligence test. Scores can vary widely around the point that may have been chosen as the cutoff for the gifted label. A student, for instance, who scores 120 on the WISC-R may actually have a "true score" of 112, well within the average range. In addition, some group tests of intelligence overidentify when selection is being done for gifted classes. This is because the test has a low ceiling, that is, it is simply not hard enough for brighter-than-average students. In particular, tests used primarily to identify developmental disabilities identify students as gifted who are simply high average.

## Hypothesis 2: *Classroom Activities Do Not Tap the Student's Intelligence*

Although intelligence tests such as the Stanford-Binet and the WISC-R are good long-term predictors of academic success, the kinds of abilities intelligence instruments measure do not necessarily correspond to those that are needed in the classroom. Most of the confusing cases of discrepancies between IQ and classroom grades are the result of comparing verbal scores with nonverbal academic performance, or performance scores or spatial-visual scores with verbal performance. A student who scores very high on the Stanford-Binet is likely to be a student with excellent verbal and reasoning abilities. However, there is little on the Stanford-Binet that can be helpful in predicting a student's artistic ability, social studies skills, or fine or gross motor skills. It is completely possible for a student to be verbally gifted but to perform poorly in situations that do not call for excellent verbal expertise. This kind of underachievement is most likely to be seen in kindergarten or the very early grades where a student's verbal precociousness may not matter as much as his or her social, physical, artistic, and musical skills. In these cases, it cannot be said that the child is not "truly" gifted; simply that the child's giftedness has not yet had an opportunity to manifest itself.

A much more common form of behavior labeled as underachievement is associated with situations where gifted students with very high scores on tests of spatial-visual abilities, such as the WISC-R performance scale or the Raven Progressive Matrices, fail to perform well in a gifted education class. Most school activities, particularly activities for gifted children, are highly verbal in nature. It is completely possible for a child to have high scores on spatial-visual tests and to be only in the average range on verbal abilities.

One of the most common scenarios for this kind of underachievement is a situation in which a child scores 140 on the WISC-R on the performance scale and 110 on the verbal scale. The full scale score will then be well in the gifted range, obscuring the fact that the student has only average verbal abilities. It is for this reason that school psychologists who have worked closely with the gifted recommend that we go well beyond the full scale score in making decisions about student placement (Hollinger & Kosek, 1986). The regular classroom and even the gifted education classroom often have little to offer the child of extraordinary spatial-visual ability. Beyond geography, geometry, art, and technical classes such as mechanical drawing and shop, the regular curriculum is oriented mostly toward the verbally gifted child. It is common that this child's unusual abilities will not be noticed, understood, or manifested in a talent area until adolescence or young adulthood. Einstein and Edison probably are examples of spatial-visual geniuses whose abilities were not tapped by schoolwork.

Counselors need to be aware that parents and teachers may have unrealistic expectations of children with high IQ scores based on high spatial-visual abilities. Counselors also need to help the students themselves reach a better understanding of the specificity of their talents. Students with spatial-visual skills need to be guided into classes in which their talents can be expressed.

### Hypothesis 3: *The Student Has Decided To Camouflage His or Her Abilities*

There are a wide variety of reasons why a student might wish to hide his or her intelligence. Intelligence tests such as the WISC-R and the Stanford-Binet are individually administered. Frequently the test administrator is warm, supportive, and engaging. A child who might otherwise be cautious about showing his or her abilities in a group situation might, with the appropriate test administrator, show skills that are normally hidden from the classroom teacher. Girls may be more likely to camouflage their abilities than boys, particularly girls who have been brought up in traditional feminine roles (Kerr, 1985). Girls are more likely to obscure their intelligence after the beginning of adolescence. Members of particular minority groups may also believe it necessary to hide ability in the classroom (Colangelo & LaFrenz, 1981). A child with a strong Black identity who feels frightened or alienated by White teachers may attempt to camouflage his or her abilities in order not to be perceived by peers as a teacher's pet. Native Americans may simply be embarrassed by the competitiveness of the classroom and not wish to humiliate others.

Counselors need to help the child who is hiding his or her abilities to find ways to "come out of hiding." Group counseling in all-female groups or groups of gifted children from the same minority group may be useful.

## High Achievement Test Scores, Low Classroom Performance

Underachievement that involves high achievement test scores and poor classroom performance differs from underachievement associated with a high IQ and low classroom performance because achievement tests are tests of knowledge and are often closely tied to curriculum. IQ tests are more general measures of reasoning, memory, and general knowledge. Therefore, a child who scores high on achievement tests is likely to possess the precise knowledge that is linked to work in school. It is difficult to explain how a child who seems indifferent or unmotivated in class can possibly have gained the knowledge necessary to score high on achievement tests. Where did the knowledge come from? Why isn't it possible for the child to show what he or she knows in class?

### Hypothesis 1: *The Tests Are Wrong*

Again, it is simply possible, given measurement error, that in rare cases achievement test scores can simply be wrong. This is likely to be the case when the achievement test scores are not extraordinarily high but merely above average. Occasionally, lucky guessing on a multiple-choice achievement test may give an unrealistic score. However, if high achievement test scores have been achieved more than once and there is a consistent pattern, this hypothesis is unlikely to be true.

### Hypothesis 2: *The Child Is Learning at Home*

Apparently, there exists a group of students who are essentially "closet learners." These are students who seem highly motivated to read at home and to practice school-related skills such as solving math problems. Why these children learn at home but seem uninterested in academic work at school can be related to a wide variety of psychological or cultural factors. Some gifted students have difficulty with authoritarian classrooms or schools and seem to underachieve in the classroom deliberately. Gowan, one of the many guidance specialists whose clinical observations support the concept of the gifted underachiever, described a "kind of intellectual delinquent who withdraws from goals, activities, and active social participation" (1957, p. 101). Although little has been written about this kind of student at the elementary and secondary levels, the "intellectual delinquent" appears often in the literature of college student development. Psychologists who work with college students have long recognized the existence of a group of students who seem uncommitted or unconnected (Katchadourian & Boli, 1985; Keniston, 1960). These students are troubling to college educators because of their apparent failure to succeed within the structure of the college environment despite their high aptitude. These students do not lack academic ability, although they may lack study skills. In many cases, the underachieving gifted student seems to be deliberately choosing to fail. This kind of underachievement represents one of the greatest challenges to the counselor.

It should also be noted that many students who earn high achievement test scores may be similar to those who achieve high IQ scores and do not perform in the classroom. That is, they may be avoiding competitiveness or attempting to avoid peer group disapproval.

## Hypothesis 3: *The Student Is Bored*

Students who have learned the material being presented in class a year or more beforehand may be too bored to perform well in class. Gifted students who have been grouped all their lives in the regular classroom may have simply given up on the possibility of being challenged. They know the material on achievement tests and may be willing to show their knowledge on tests, but are too angry or depressed about the repetitiousness and dullness of classroom work to pretend interest. Some of these students may actually try very hard to attain high scores on achievement tests purely for the surprise value. They may enjoy puzzling teachers and counselors with their high scores. Whereas the "intellectual delinquents" mentioned in the second hypothesis are rebelling against authority, these underachievers are rebelling against boredom. Despite the fact that these students seem beyond the reach of counselors or teachers, their kind of underachievement may be the most easily cured. Extraordinary academic challenge seems to be the treatment of choice. Often these students are hungry for any teacher or class that will provide them with new knowledge, new skills, and the opportunity to work hard at learning.

## High Grade Point Average, Low Classroom Performance

This kind of underachievement, which is based on a difference between a cumulative, unstandardized measure of ability and performance at a particular point in time, is often observed during transitional periods from elementary to junior high, from junior to senior high, or from senior high to college. A student who previously had an unblemished record of A's suddenly seems to be unable to do better than C work. Teachers are often particularly alarmed by students with this pattern because of their seemingly precipitous decline in abilities.

### Hypothesis 1: *Standards Have Been Lower in Previous Schooling*

Gifted students who change schools or who are making transitions in school from one level to another may show this pattern if the expectations of the previous school were simply not as high as those of the present school. There is a certain momentum that gathers behind the student who receives excellent marks in the early grades. Teachers in each consecutive grade, having spoken with previous teachers, may assume that the child is bright and highly achieving and mark that child accordingly even when the abilities may not be as high as presumed. Only when the student encounters a teacher who does not have access to previous records or to former teachers do the grades decline.

It should also be no surprise that grades decline when a student moves from a regular classroom to a gifted classroom or changes from a regular school or a magnet school to a school for the gifted. Faced with much greater competition, many students will no longer be straight-A students. This is not a true case of underachievement, but simply a case of students performing at their true ability level in an environment of students with similar and greater abilities.

## Hypothesis 2: *Situational Factors Are Interfering With Academic Performance*

Like with all children, gifted children's academic performance is affected by trouble at home. Family conflict or divorce, substance abuse in the home, spouse and child abuse, or illness or death of a family member are all possible causes of a decline in academic performance. Webb, Meckstroth, and Tolan (1982) observed that gifted children seem to be much more sensitive than average children to conflict and loss. Therefore, any of these home situations may cause drastic changes in the gifted child's behavior at school. Although many gifted children continue to do well in school despite crises in the home, for most of them school becomes just one more source of stress. Poor classroom performance may actually be a cry for help. The gifted student, aware of his or her reputation as an excellent scholar, may be counting on the counselor to notice the change in his or her grades, to comment upon them, and to offer help and support.

## High Classroom Performance, Low Achievement Test or IQ Scores

Although sometimes labeled as underachievement, this is not technically underachieving behavior. Actual performance that is higher than that predicted by psychological measures is sometimes called overachievement. There are several reasons why students' actual academic performance may be better than what was predicted by IQ or achievement test scores.

## Hypothesis 1: *The Student Has Test Anxiety*

There are students who, under individual or group testing conditions, become so anxious that they cannot perform up to their true ability levels. Students may be test-anxious because of overly high expectations of others, learning disabilities that interfere with performance on particular types of tests, or frightening past experiences with test taking. True test anxiety goes far beyond nervousness or heightened arousal before the test. Test-anxious individuals become physically ill, lose all capacity to remember information, and experience extreme symptoms of stress such as trembling, sweating, dryness of the mouth, and lack of concentration.

It is likely that test anxiety not only affects the performance of text-anxious students on standardized intelligence or achievement tests but also on classroom tests. Therefore, the discrepancy between high classroom performance and low test scores should occur only among students who have been educated in schools or classrooms where little in-class testing is done.

Because past grades are the best predictors of future grades, when grades are high and test scores are low, it is probably best simply to ignore the test scores. However, in cases in which it is apparent that low achievement test scores will significantly interfere with a student's chances of entering a gifted program or a particular college, it may be necessary for counselors to help students alleviate test anxiety through relaxation training or desensitization procedures.

## Hypothesis 2: *The Student Is Benefiting From a Reputation or Halo Effect*

Occasionally, when a student's grades are much better than his or her achievement test scores, the student is benefiting either from family reputation or personal reputation. It is a common complaint of younger brothers and sisters that teachers are constantly comparing them to their older siblings. In many cases, however, these comparisons can be advantageous. When an older sibling or whole line of siblings has been highly achieving in school, teachers come to have extremely high expectations of any family member. Sometimes students are graded somewhat leniently and given the benefit of the doubt because it is simply assumed that being from the same family of high achievers, this student, too, is one of unusual ability. Only when the student goes to a larger school where his or her siblings or family may not be known or to a new school where the family is unknown will grades begin to match achievement test scores more closely.

A student may also have extraordinary social skills that allow him or her to build a reputation as a high achiever not in keeping with the student's actual accumulation of knowledge and skills in the classroom. A student who is personable, lively, and an active participant in class may be perceived as intelligent and knowledgeable even when his or her actual recall and understanding of curriculum materials are not better than average. Achievement tests will nearly always show a discrepancy between what the student seems to know and what the student actually knows. This kind of overachievement may be particularly frustrating to teachers and counselors whose liking for an interpersonally skilled student causes them to be unhappy with the results of achievement tests. When test scores prevent the student from access to a gifted program or to a chosen college, it is a particularly sore point with those teachers and counselors who support the student's abilities. In these cases, retesting is always a good policy; however, when tests consistently show that the student is average or less than average in his or her understanding of particular curriculum materials, it is probably not a good idea to expect that student to be able to succeed in more challenging work.

## Interventions for Underachievement

It is apparent from the above discussion that there are many causes of underachievement and many cases in which classroom behavior does not match test results. It is important, then, to understand that there must be as many types of interventions as there are types of discrepancies. What follows are strategies ranging from the simplest to the most complex.

## Retesting or Reinterpreting Tests

In several cases described above, discrepancies were the result of test error. When this hypothesis may be true, it is important that a student be retested, preferably with a parallel form of the same test. Also, when it is likely that the test has been misinterpreted, counselors should seek an expert opinion concerning complex results. It may be possible simply by consulting the test manual to determine how the test could be misinterpreted. Occasionally it may be necessary to call a school psychologist, clinical psychologist, or counseling psychologist with expertise in measurement in order to understand particularly puzzling results. It is important to remember that even most psychologists do not have training in interpreting the results of intelligence or achievement tests for gifted students. Therefore, the psychologist consulted should have some coursework and pratice in gifted education.

Occasionally it is the policy of a school district to allow only a limited amount of testing and no retesting. In this case it will probably be necessary for counselors to suggest that parents seek private testing and interpretation from a psychologist. This can be expensive and time-consuming for the parents and the student, but the benefits may be great if the student can then be appropriately placed in the academic program that he or she needs.

## Appropriate Academic Placement

Many problems related to underachievement and overachievement can be solved by appropriate academic placement. Frequently more elaborate interventions such as time management and study skills training as well as personal counseling are tried rather than the simpler solution of appropriate academic placement. This is because a gifted underachiever's behavior is so markedly similar to that of a student who is having trouble with work habits or whose personal problems are interfering with academic work that it is assumed that these interventions must be attempted. Nevertheless, a great many underachievers will promptly begin to achieve when they are placed in a more challenging environment. Bored, restless, and resentful, many gifted underachievers are simply turned off to classroom activities.

Robert Sawyer, Director of the Talent Identification Program at Duke University, observed that intellectual challenge was often the treatment of choice for students who had been identified by talent search procedures as highly gifted, but were not achieving in their home school. Often these underachieving gifted students were being forced to sit in classrooms where the level of instruction was 4 or 5 years behind their actual abilities. This is not to say that a student who has been inappropriately placed in the regular classroom may not also need counseling or help with study skills. Many years of boredom can create a wide variety of emotional and behavioral problems.

Various combinations of placement and counseling should probably be tried at different school levels. For example, a gifted child in early primary school who is showing signs of underachievement may benefit simply from being advanced in the appropriate academic areas. The child can be moved to a higher reading group or allowed to skip a grade. In later primary grades, it may become necessary to combine some helping interventions with appropriate placement. Joanne Whitmore's (1980) Underachieving Gifted program in the Cupertino Public Schools provided challenge while at the same time making available support groups and counseling for low self-esteem, depression, and school-related difficulties. At the Guidance Laboratory for Gifted and Talented at the University of Nebraska, a successful technique was to radically accelerate junior high gifted underachievers into college courses. Junior high seems to be a critical time for highly gifted students in which, if given appropriate challenge, they are able to advance rapidly in their learning and development; however, if they lack challenge, they may become rebellious or withdrawn. Enrolling junior high students in upper-level high school courses or even college courses may give the underachieving gifted student a new start. For the underachieving gifted student in high school who seems to be increasingly cynical and bored, early admission to college may be the best option. Frequently, it is sufficient for students to graduate with a minimum number of credits or even to complete a high school graduation equivalency exam to move on to college. Although it seems paradoxical to accelerate a student who is doing poorly, adding challenge to the student's life may be more effective than any number of counseling interventions.

## Counseling Interventions

Despite the success of appropriate placement as an intervention for underachieving gifted students, some students still will require short-term or long-term counseling in order to improve their academic performance. Sometimes these are the underachieving students who have personality disorders or behavior disorders above and beyond the realm of boredom and lack of challenge. Students who are underachieving because of depression, substance abuse, family difficulties, or other conflicts are likely to need more than appropriate placement. On the other hand, some underachieving students who need counseling are simply students who have been frustrated for so long by the lack of challenge in their education that they have become embittered and pessimistic about the possibility of ever loving learning again. Many of these students could be considered to be suffering from existential depression, characterized by alienation and a sense of meaninglessness. Attentive, short-term counseling interventions aimed at the development of purpose and meaning can be particularly effective with this latter group.

A counseling intervention designed to help underachieving high school and college students to discover a sense of meaning and purpose was developed at The University of Iowa's Counseling Laboratory for Talent

Development. This workshop is a variation of the career counseling workshop presented in chapter 5 on counseling for multipotentiality. The steps, as designed by Arcenaux and Kerr (1989) for the Counseling Laboratory for Talent Development, are included in the chapter 3 Resources section at the end of the book. This intervention is currently being evaluated in terms of its effectiveness in helping students to set goals, improve academic performance, and increase their sense of identity and purpose.

## Summary

Although gifted underachievers seem to have more in common with underachievers in general than with other gifted students, there are important differences. Underachieving gifted students may be socially immature, may experience more emotional problems, may engage in antisocial behavior, and may have low self-concepts. However, it is also likely that they have a deep need for understanding the world and themselves, a thirst for knowledge, and the capacity to change negative behaviors when intellectually challenged. The counselor should test the full range of hypotheses about underachieving behavior before choosing an intervention. Interventions include retesting, academic placement, and counseling. Existential counseling focusing on the discovery of meaning and purpose may be helpful.

## References

Anastasi, A. (1976). *Psychological testing*. New York: Macmillan.

Arcenaux, C. (1990). *Personality characteristics, interests, and values of differentially achieving able college students*. Unpublished doctoral dissertation, The University of Iowa, Iowa City, IA.

Arcenaux, C., & Kerr, B. (1989). *Intervention for underachivers*. Unpublished manuscript. Belin National Center for Gifted Education, Iowa City, IA.

Bricklin, B., & Bricklin, P. (1967). *Bright child, poor grades*. New York: Delacorte Press.

Colangelo, N., & LaFrenz, N. (1981). Counseling the culturally diverse gifted. *Gifted Child Quarterly, 25*, 27–30.

Colangelo, N., & Pfleger, L. R. (1979). Academic self-concept of gifted high school students. In N. Colangelo & R. Zaffrann (Eds.), *New voices in counseling the gifted*. Dubuque, IA: Kendall-Hunt.

Dowdall, C. B., & Colangelo, N. (1982). Underachieving gifted students: Review and implications. *Gifted Child Quarterly*, 26(4), 179–184.

Fine, M., & Pitts, R. (1980). Intervention with underachieving gifted children: Rationale and strategies. *Gifted Child Quarterly*, 24, 51–55.

Gowan, J. C. (1957). Dynamics of underachievement of gifted children. *Exceptional Children*, 24, 98–101.

Hecht, K. A. (1975). Teacher ratings of potential dropouts and academically gifted children: Are they related? *Journal of Teacher Education*, 26, 172–175.

Hollinger, C. L., & Kosek, S. (1986). Beyond the use of full scale I.Q. scores. *Gifted Child Quarterly*, 30(2), 74–77.

Katchadourian, H. A., & Boli, J. (1985). *Careerism and intellectualism among college students*. San Francisco: Jossey-Bass.

Keniston, K. (1960). *The uncommitted: Alienated youth in American society*. New York: Harcourt, Brace, Jovanovich.

Kerr, B. A. (1985). *Smart girls, gifted women*. Columbus, OH: Ohio Psychology.

Pringle, M. L. (1970). *Able misfits*. London: Longman Group.

Rimm, S. (1986). *The underachievement syndrome*. Watertown, WI: Apple.

Webb, J. T., Meckstroth, E. A., & Tolan, S. S. (1982). *Guiding the gifted child*. Columbus, OH: Ohio Psychology.

Whitmore, J. R. (1980). *Giftedness, conflict, and underachievement*. Boston: Allyn & Bacon.

# College Planning for Gifted Students

One of the most important decisions the counselor will assist the gifted student in making is the choice of a college. Bright students and their parents often have strong, and sometimes conflicting, opinions about college choices. There are over 3,000 colleges and universities in the United States, all vying for the enrollment of bright students. Matching students and colleges is a difficult task particularly when it is nearly impossible for any counselor to know the characteristics of more institutions than those within their own state and a few outside their own state.

Most of the information available to counselors and students is in the form of college brochures and pamphlets. These materials, sent by the colleges and universities themselves, tend to be characterized by advertising rather than objective reporting of information about the institution. Many college rating guides exist; however, few of these guides are objective and comprehensive. In addition to the problem of the scarcity of information about colleges is the fact that gifted students are often unsure of their own characteristics and the ways in which their needs might be met by various kinds of higher education institutions. Finally, students, parents, and counselors are all often hampered by misconceptions of generalizations about what kind of college is best for gifted students.

## Misconceptions About College Planning for the Gifted

One of the most common misconceptions about gifted students' choice of a college is the idea that all bright students should be guided toward Ivy League institutions. Parents often worry that their child will not get into Harvard or Yale if his or her grade point average dips below 4.0. Many parents and educators seem to believe that Harvard, Yale, and other Ivy League schools are somehow an extension of gifted education programming in high school. This is not the case, however. For some bright students the highly competitive academic environments of Ivy League colleges are stimulating and exciting. There is no doubt that these colleges are academically competitive, because the nature of their admissions policies ensures that most students who enter are in the 95th percentile of academic achievement. Even the brightest students on a typical state university campus in the Midwest would only be slightly above average among student populations of Ivy League schools. Although these schools provide an opportunity for gifted students to interact with their intellectual peers, sometimes, for the first time, students may experience difficulty from having to go from the top of the class to the middle or the bottom. Gifted students who plan to attend Ivy League colleges should not only have good grades and high achievement test scores, but also high self-esteem and a strong sense of self-confidence.

In addition to being aware of the competitiveness of Ivy League schools, students should also take into account the degree of individualized attention they are likely to receive. At Ivy League institutions, bright students are common and professors are unlikely to take a special interest in a student merely because of his or her excellent high school achievements. By contrast, at large midwestern state institutions and moderately competitive liberal arts colleges, there are faculty members who actively seek out gifted students for collaboration and mentoring. The tight employment market for professors in the 1970s and 1980s ensures that there are extraordinarily talented faculty members at institutions everywhere throughout the United States and at almost every level of quality. Brilliant, underemployed professors make eager mentors for gifted students. It is not a matter of taking one's chances that a non-Ivy League school might have appropriate faculty and coursework. Instead, for the bright student who has well-defined goals and areas of interest, it may be useful to discover where in the nation the leading scholars in his or her area of interest are currently employed. Contacting these scholars, no matter where they are teaching, could be the first step in discovering a college or university where a student may be able to receive individualized attention.

Another misconception about college planning for gifted students is that all colleges and universities are looking for well-rounded students who have high grades in all courses and many extracurricular activities. Most colleges and universities are well aware of the difficulties that multipotential gifted students have in selecting a major and narrowing down goals. Three or four inches of fine print under the gifted student's picture in the yearbook is no longer considered the best indicator of the student's potential for success in college. In fact, students with too many extracurricular activities in high school may risk a decline in academic achievement in college if they try to continue the same level of out-of-class involvement. Therefore, colleges and universities are interested in students with moderately active life-styles and focused energies. A student who has pursued three or four extracurricular activities closely related to his or her potential college major or area of academic interest is likely to be seen as a better integrated and more mature student.

Another misconception among gifted students is that a 4.0 grade point average is absolutely necessary for all the "best" colleges. As will be seen in the next section, most colleges want students who have achieved good grades in rigorous coursework. A B+ average on a high school transcript made up of content-oriented honors courses and advanced courses may be seen as more positive than an A average in an unchallenging, light program.

## What Do Colleges Want?

Although there are as many answers to this question as there are colleges, some generalizations can be made. First of all, colleges want students who will graduate. The best predictor of college grades are high school grades (Astin, 1987). Therefore, the high school grade point average is an important part of the formula used to predict college student success.

However, no colleges recruit only 4.0 or straight-A students. Instead, colleges are interested in a consistent pattern of high grades. It is assumed that even the best students are likely to receive some grades lower than A's, particularly in nonacademic courses. Few admissions officers are interested in students whose high grade point averages are the result of taking the easiest courses available.

One additional component of most formulae used to predict success in college is the achievement test score. Usually the scores from the SAT and the ACT are used in combination with the grade point average to predict the success of a student. The college admissions exam is not merely a measure of abstract aptitude for college work; it is also a measure of the rigorousness and thoroughness of the student's course taking. The admissions exams differ slightly in their orientation. The makers of the SAT claim that their test is more of a measure of aptitude, that is, mathematical and verbal reasoning skills, and the makers of the ACT explain that their exam is more curriculum-based. Colleges and universities on the East Coast and the West Coast are more likely to use the results of the SAT exam, whereas colleges in the Midwest are more likely to use the results of the ACT exam. Major college admissions and advanced placement tests, along with addresses, are in the Resources section of the book.

Colleges and universities also ask for an application that usually includes essays or statements of purpose, three or more letters of recommendation, and occasionally other supporting evidence. Each institution of higher education has its own unique system for assigning values to the grade point average, the admissions test score, and supporting documents. Although grade point average and admissions exam scores together are the best predictors of success in college, recommendations and applications give admissions officers some sense of the student's character. From these documents, admissions officers hope to learn if the prospective student possesses other qualities besides the chances of succeeding, such as a potential for leadership and a probability that the student will behave ethically and legally.

Gifted students, then, are best advised to work for a meaningfully high grade point average; to prepare both through coursework and study for admissions exams; and to gather documentation that will attest to their good character and potential for being involved and enthusiastic members of the university community.

## Planning for College*

Sandra Berger, in her excellent book, *College Planning for Gifted Students* (1989), suggested a college planning time line that begins in *seventh grade*. Seventh grade, according to Berger, is a time for students to explore their community and discover the resources available to help with planning for college. In addition, seventh grade is a time to search for summer programs outside the community that are oriented toward the needs of gifted students. Within the community, seventh-grade gifted students should explore high school magnet schools, opportunities to obtain high school credit, and places to participate in volunteer work. Summer programs sponsored by regional talent searches, universities, and schools are an excellent way to meet other gifted students as well as to discover what it is like to live and work on a college campus. A student and his or her parents should shop around not only for the best bargain in a summer program but also for the program that will provide the most stimulating intellectual experiences and college preparatory experiences.

*Eighth grade*, according to Berger, is the time for the gifted student to develop a master plan, including an academic plan and a time management plan. An academic plan includes all courses required for high school graduation and elective courses, and a time management plan is essentially a life-style planning procedure for assigning the number of hours that will be needed for class homework, extracurricular interests, recreation, and family activities. Eighth grade is also a good time to begin investigating career options. Career interest tests and computer-assisted career guidance programs are available to many students. Occasionally, however, it will be necessary for junior high students to go to a high school guidance counselor or an independent counselor for this preliminary career exploration. This is also a time to continue volunteer work, experiment with new courses, and be involved in extracurricular activities. Summer programs may also follow the eighth-grade year, perhaps as a continuation of a summer program entered the year before or a new one on another college campus.

Berger advises that in *ninth grade*, parents, student, and counselor meet as a group to plan for the student's next 4 years. This planning

---

*From *College Planning for Gifted Students* by Sandra L. Berger, 1989, Reston, VA: The Council for Exceptional Children. Reprinted by permission.

group should review the 4-year high school plan, examining which courses might be required for high school as well as various colleges, gaps in the high school offerings that need to be uncovered, and strategies for filling those gaps either through summer programs or out-of-school tutoring. Extracurricular activities should be discussed, and finally, financial planning for college should begin at this point. If the family expects the student to be working in order to pay for part of the college costs, then the type of work and the length of hours should be discussed at this time. Ninth grade is also a time to become familiar with the high school career center and to explore career opportunities in depth. It is probably time for the multipotential student to begin focusing on several extracurricular activities rather than many and to engage in some focused volunteer work.

Berger advises that all gifted students take the Preliminary Scholastic Aptitude Test (PSAT) in October of their *10th-grade* year. Students should take the PSAT mainly as practice, because scores do not count during the 11th-grade year. However, in 11th grade PSAT scores will be used for the National Merit Scholarship Qualifying Test, and it is best for students to be familiar with the types of questions and the nature of the exam. Tenth grade, according to Berger, is also a good time to become familiar with college reference books such as The College Entrance Examination Board's *College Handbook, An Index of Majors.* Counselors may need to guide students through the process of reviewing college reference books because there are so many subjectively organized types of books. Tenth grade is a good time for college visitation, at least for nearby colleges. Berger also advises that gifted high school students take achievement tests at the end of the 10th grade in any subject in which they have done well but are not planning to continue studying, such as foreign languages. Because only three achievement tests are given per session, it is important to take several tests each year if possible. In the 10th grade volunteer work should continue, but Berger also advises that the students consider an internship, travel, or working with an adult who has an interesting career. Career planning can now involve career interest inventories and personality tests. These may be available in high school or at a nearby college or university.

*Eleventh grade* may be the most important year for college planning for gifted students. This is the year in which the PSAT is given in October. PSAT scores will be used for the National Merit Scholarship Qualifying

Test. It is also important for 11th graders to sign up to take SATs or ACTs in the spring. Determine which colleges prefer ACTs and which colleges prefer SATs. Berger suggests that if SAT scores are not as high as expected, a preparatory course may be helpful during junior year. More standardized achievement tests should be taken during this year. Advanced placement tests can also be taken during junior year if advanced placement preparation courses have been taken. Because the junior year grade point average may be particularly important to colleges, this is the year when gifted students should concentrate on their academic work. Financial planning should also continue at this point.

Junior year is the time for serious, in-depth exploration of colleges. Berger suggests developing a list of 10 to 20 colleges and working up a comparison chart. This chart should include size, geographic location, course offerings, costs, available scholarships, extracurricular activities, and selectivity. College visits should also begin in junior year if they have not begun already. Anytime the family takes a trip, visits to colleges should be included in that area of the country. Berger suggests visiting several different kinds of colleges—large and small, public and private. During the summer of the junior year, attending another summer institute for the gifted and talented is a good idea. It is particularly important to go to a university-based summer school. Alternatively, a summer internship, travel abroad, or college planning seminars can be useful during this last summer. By the summer of the junior year, gifted students should have requested application forms from about 10 colleges.

*Twelfth grade* marks the year of decision for gifted students. Many college representatives will be available at college nights and other high school visitations. Berger suggests that students make a file of every college they are considering that includes such important information as application deadlines, financial aid deadlines, notification dates, tests required, costs, recommendations required, and interview deadlines. Any recommendations not yet gathered should be sought during the early part of the senior year. SATs and ACTs should be taken if they have not yet been taken or if a retake is desired. Also, the final achievement tests should be taken during this year.

Students should have SAT and ACT scores sent to their counselor and to the schools to which they are applying. Counselors and students should go over the scores together and arrive at an appropriate interpretation. Berger suggests that students be sure to understand their high school's procedure for sending out transcripts, letters of recommendation, and other materials. It is important that the school's calendar match that of the colleges with early deadlines. Gifted students can often benefit from adding supporting materials to their file in the form of descriptions of courses, descriptions of special opportunities, and explanations of gifted program offerings. Wherever it is possible to have interviews with admissions counselors from colleges and universities, it is important to sign up because the interview may be a deciding factor.

Students should also take time during senior year to prepare the application essay. Any help that guidance counselors and teachers can give is important. Finally, guidance counselors, students, and parents need to work closely together on the actual college decision during the period in the spring when most colleges need to be notified. Time should be set aside for a formal decision-making process. A method for making a decision that includes criteria and goals should be devised by parents, counselor, and student. Once the decision is made, further exploration should include information about orientation courses, registration, and use of advanced placement and other credit.

## What Do Gifted Students Want From a College?

Much of the concentration of students and their parents during the last year of high school is on the question, "What do colleges want?" However, it is important to ask, "What do gifted students want from their colleges and universities?" This is the question that Nicholas Colangelo and I have been asking in our ACT studies of students at the 90th, 95th, and 99th percentiles, and of perfect scorers (Colangelo & Kerr, 1990; Kerr & Colangelo, 1988).

One of the major concerns of bright students is whether a college or university has an honors program. Honors programs at colleges and universities serve several purposes for bright students. First, and most important, honors programs provide courses that are usually more challenging and more rigorous than other courses at the university. In addition, interdisciplinary and innovative courses are likely to be offered through the honors program. Second, honors programs usually provide smaller classes and more opportunities for individualized instruction with professors. At a large university, instructors in an honors program are more likely to be professors than graduate students. Finally, honors programs, particularly at large universities, can provide the experience of a college within a college. Often students who participate in an honors program at a large university get to know each other well, have many classes together, and have the opportunity to form friendships with intellectually oriented students like themselves.

For all these reasons, gifted students find honors programs very attractive. It may be that gifted students are under the impression that honors programs will simply be a continuation of gifted education in high school. However, college honors programs do not tend to follow the structure or methods of secondary school gifted programs. Honors programs at universities focus much more on academic rigor and much less on enrichment activities such as group problem solving or special events. Although honors coursework is usually more difficult than regular coursework at the university, special grades or points are not always assigned. In college as in high school, however, grade point average should not be the primary consideration in determining which courses to take.

In addition to their fondness for honors programs, bright students in our ACT studies showed a special interest in extracurricular activities. Apparently, bright students want to be very involved in campus life. In fact, the pattern of anticipated extracurricular activities that academically talented students in our ACT studies showed, proved that the image of the gifted student in college as a reclusive uninvolved "bookworm" was completely untrue. The more accomplished that students were in achievement test scores, the more likely they were to want to be involved in campus activities. Compared to average students, bright students wanted more involvement in student government, student publications such as yearbooks and newspapers, and special interest and departmental clubs. Departmental clubs were one of the highest-rated activities among bright students. It may be a surprise to counselors and college admissions personnel to learn how desirable these kinds of activities are to students. Such organizations as a French language circle, a physics club, or psychology students' organizations such as Psi Chi have a particular interest for bright students. The only activities in which the brightest students have less interest than do average students are such activities as Greek organizations, sports, and religious activities. Even though these students show less interest than do average students in these activities, however, their interest levels in them are still quite high.

Finally, bright students have a special interest in career counseling. Although our studies show that for the most part bright students seem to reject personal counseling, they see career counseling as highly desirable. Many gifted students enter college undecided about their college major and seem to feel some pressure to make a decision early. In addition, they often are future-oriented and want to spend time thinking about what particular course choices might mean for their long-term goals.

Gifted students' strong interest in career counseling may go beyond a concern for making major and career decisions. Many bright students, by the time they are preparing for college, realize that they have values decisions to make. These students like to discuss the ways in which they are developing purpose and meaning in their lives, but they do not wish to do this in the context of personal counseling, which is somehow stigmatized as being for people with psychological problems. Instead, gifted students seek developmental counseling—that is, counseling that helps "normal" people achieve self-actualization rather than counseling that focuses on remediation of problems. Colleges with strong student development philosophies are likely to be those that provide developmental counseling for bright students.

## College Majors

One of the most distressing findings of our ACT studies of bright students is that bright students today are extremely narrow in their choice of a college major. We studied the career goals of the very highest-scoring students on the ACT, those in the 95th and 99th percentiles. We found that when given the choice of 196 possible college majors, half of the students were crowding into just five majors: pre-medicine, engineering, business, pre-law, and communications. Clearly, gifted students have only the most stereotyped notions of what kinds of majors are appropriate for them. Even the perfect scorers had a tendency to choose the same majors that average and above-average students choose. Fewer than 2% of those students who scored perfectly on the English subtests of the ACT were contemplating English majors; fewer than 3% who scored perfectly in math were considering majors in pure mathematics; and only 12% of those students with perfect scores in the natural sciences were planning to enter pure science majors such as biology, physics, or astronomy. Of the 577 students who scored perfectly in social studies, only 2 were anticipating majoring in history (Colangelo & Kerr, 1990). Apparently, gifted students have not had access to information about careers in academic areas and very few are considering careers in higher education despite the excellent opportunities and many projected openings in that area in the 1990s and beyond. Therefore, a great many gifted students entering college will need academic guidance and career counseling to make appropriate choices.

## The College Needs of Women

College planning for gifted young women may involve seeking the college or university that can deal with their special needs. There is some evidence that gifted women may fare better at women's colleges. To illustrate, more women scholars and leaders are graduates of women's colleges than of coeducational institutions. Apparently, women's colleges allow more leadership opportunities for gifted women than do coeducational colleges, where women's needs often come second.

Many concerns about gifted women in coeducational institutions are related to the findings of those commissions that have studied the role of women on college campuses in America today. The landmark study of women on campus, *Out of the Classroom: A Chilly Climate for Women* (Hall & Sandler, 1984), found that women continue to receive an inferior education compared to that of men in coeducational colleges and universities. College men receive more scholarships, fellowships, and opportunities for mentoring. Even more disturbing, college men are called on three times more often in the classroom by their professors. In addition, women students suffer from sexual harassment, sexist jokes, and general neglect in their development as scholars. Compared to men, women students achieve fewer leadership positions in student government and student newspapers, and they seem to be less involved than men in college life in general.

Although women's liberation has changed the face of the world, much remains to be done on the college campus. Until women and men receive equal treatment in the college classroom and on the campus, it may be that women's colleges provide the most supportive and intellectually stimulating environment for gifted young women.

Finally, some evidence shows that gifted young women continue to choose college majors from a narrower field than do college men. Although talented college women are now choosing majors in pre-medicine and pre-law and business as frequently as are young gifted men, they continue to avoid engineering and the hard sciences. Gifted women gravitate toward the biological sciences when their interests and abilities qualify them well for any scientific field. Gifted young women also may avoid some college majors in which they are truly interested because of their fears of sex-role stereotyping. Important examples are teaching and nursing; many gifted women are attracted to these professions but are concerned that the choice of teaching or nursing will be disputed by parents or teachers who want to guide them toward nontraditional occupations.

## The College Needs of Minority Gifted Students

Gifted students of color who are planning for college face a disturbing paradox. On the one hand, colleges and universities throughout the nation are competing vigorously for the enrollment of talented minority students. The small numbers of minority students who score in the higher percentiles on achievement tests become the targets for vast quantities of recruiting materials for higher education institutions. At the same time, however, reports of the revival or continuation of racism on college and university campuses are frightening to bright minority students and their parents (Laney, 1990). In addition to outright racism, students of color are often deeply aware that they will be part of an isolated, small group of students of their ethnicity on many college campuses. Colleges that do an excellent job of recruiting minority students often do not follow up with well-thought-out plans for retaining those students. An academically gifted Black student may arrive on a college campus to learn that the other Black students are spread out one or two to a floor in the residence halls in order to ''create diversity.'' They may be exposed to both covert and overt resentment from majority students who believe that their selection or financial aid has been unfairly earned. They may be stereotyped as having needs for remedial work or basic courses even when they are qualified for the most rigorous honors coursework. Feeling alone and resented, many minority students see little reason to stay at the college that once recruited them so intensely. Seldom have procedures been set for retention counseling or exit interviews.

Thus, many of the most promising and brilliant young minority students are lost to American higher education. Counselors who wish to help students of color make effective college decisions need to help the students look beyond the basic characteristics of colleges and universities to discover the degree to which a particular college supports its minority students, develops effective retention programs, provides for caring communities, and displays appreciation of cultural diversity. That minority students are particularly interested in support services, counseling, and encouragement to participate in a wide range of activities was demonstrated by a recent study of minority students scoring in the 95th percentile on the ACT exams (Kerr, Colangelo, Maxey, & Christensen, in press). The presence of a Black Culture House or Latino Student Center is not a guarantee of an appreciation of cultural diversity. Students of color should look for higher education institutions that have shown a pattern of nondiscrimination over many years, a pattern of a nonracist student culture, and a pattern of affirmative action policies that have ensured strong proportions of faculty members of color.

Little in the way of academic and career guidance exists for the gifted minority student. Often students of color are aggressively recruited by particular academic departments, leading to strong proportions of students of color in particular areas of the campus. Too often, this means that students choose a major such as law or engineering only because of the presence of large numbers of students in their ethnic group in those particular areas. Counselors need to ensure that minority gifted students are aware of the full array of options before them. Counselors should help gifted minority students to make sense of the recruitment letters and brochures and to discover among all the information with which they are bombarded those facts that will help them make effective college and major decisions.

## Summary

To plan for college effectively, gifted students need to understand what colleges expect and to understand their own needs. Counselors should help gifted students and their parents by sharing a time line for planning and encouraging them to set and meet goals according to that time line. Gifted students may need to be encouraged to be more risk-taking in their choice of a college major; too many bright students restrict themselves to "practical" majors. Women and minority gifted students should be careful to select colleges that are aware and supportive of their special needs.

## References

Astin, A., Green, K., Korn, W. S., & Schalit, M. (1987). *The American freshman. National norms for Fall of 1987.* Los Angeles: Higher Education Research Institute.

Berger, S. L. (1989). *College planning for gifted students.* Reston, VA: ERIC/ CEC Clearinghouse on Gifted and Handicapped Children.

Colangelo, N., & Kerr, B. A. (1990). Extreme academic talent: Profiles of perfect scorers. *Journal of Educational Psychology, 82,* 404–409.

Hall, R. M., & Sandler, B. R. (1984). *Out of the classroom: A chilly campus climate for women?* Washington, DC: Project on the Status and Education of Women.

Kerr, B. A., & Colangelo, N. (1988). College plans of academically talented students. *Journal of Counseling and Development, 67*(1), 42–49.

Kerr, B. A., Colangelo, N., Maxey, J., & Christensen, P. (in press). Characteristics of academically talented minority students. *Journal of Counseling and Development.*

Laney, J. T. (1990, April 10). Why tolerate campus bigots? *New York Times.*

Why do individuals of remarkable intellectual potential often fail to fulfill the promise of their youth?* Even Terman's highly gifted subjects often were found to have had great difficulty translating their extraordinary intellectual ability into meaningful, productive work. Over half of the gifted women became homemakers despite earlier career aspirations; and even those who eventually achieved satisfaction and success had had difficulty deciding among many career options (Terman & Oden, 1935; 1947). More recent clinical case studies and research on the gifted show that the path from youthful talent to adult accomplishment is not always straight and smooth. National Merit Scholars (Watley, 1969), Presidential Scholars (Kaufmann, 1981), and graduates of major learning programs (Kerr, 1985) all have been found to experience problems in career decision making or life planning.

# Career Counseling for Gifted and Talented Students

---

* The introduction to this chapter is adapted from Kerr, B. A. (1989). *Counseling Gifted Students*. Indianapolis, IN: Indiana State Department of Education.

There are, of course, a wide variety of possible explanations for career indecision and vocational dissatisfaction among young gifted adults. This chapter will describe the consequences of having too many choices, too narrow interests, or poor decision-making skills.

One missing ingredient in the development of most gifted individuals is career guidance. Although special educational programs exist for about one third of the gifted in the nation's schools (Cox, Daniel, & Boston, 1985), few include a guidance career component. Most career interventions with gifted and talented students have been developed by universities and colleges as a part of counselor education programs, counseling centers, and career centers (Roper & Berry, 1986).

This chapter presents techniques for career counseling with gifted students that draw upon effective strategies used at the Wisconsin Guidance Institute for Talented Students, the Guidance Laboratory for Gifted and Talented at the University of Nebraska, and the Counseling Laboratory for Talent Development at The University of Iowa.

## Multipotentiality

Multipotentiality is the cause of most gifted students' difficulties in career development (Kerr, 1981). Multipotentiality is defined as the ability to select and develop any number of competencies at a high level (Frederickson & Rothney, 1972). Gifted students and those who are concerned with their guidance have long recognized that having multiple potentials can be a mixed blessing. Without appropriate career guidance, multipotentiality may become a curse.

A multipotential student may take a vocational test only to learn that he or she is "similar" in interests and abilities to biologists, librarians, musicians, reporters, English teachers, and ministers. Attaining straight A's and uniformly high achievement test scores means that the student cannot make decisions based on what he or she "does best." After graduation from high school, the multipotential student may vacillate between career choices, delaying career decisions until financial need and the end of a nonfocused education drive the student to take a job by default. As an adult, the multipotential gifted individual may dabble in a series of jobs, finding success but little satisfaction in any. Parents, teachers, and counselors are puzzled throughout the disappointing and spotty career of the multipotential individual. They continue to insist,

"But you could be anything you want to be!" not understanding that this is precisely the problem.

What research evidence exists about the problem of multipotentiality? The evidence is available from several areas of investigation regarding giftedness: analyses of case studies of gifted and talented students, longitudinal studies of career patterns, and analyses of vocational interests (Kerr, 1981).

Some of the best case studies demonstrating the difficulties of multipotential gifted youth were those that Leta Hollingworth conducted in the 1920s. Hollingworth (1926) interviewed hundreds of gifted children during her career in an attempt to build a knowledge base of the "nature and nurture of genius." She found that gifted students were typically capable of so many different kinds of success that they had difficulty in confining themselves to a "reasonable number of enterprises." Hollingworth felt that gifted students experiencing these problems had a need for understanding and guidance that was severely neglected.

The Wisconsin Guidance Institute for Talented Students provided individualized guidance for gifted students from 1957 to 1984. Many individuals of that institute and their research associates at other institutions contributed to the definition and understanding of multipotentiality (Colangelo & Zaffrann, 1979; Frederickson & Rothney, 1972; Sanborn, 1979). Perrone, Karshner, and Male (1979), summarizing observations from the guidance of gifted young people, observed that being told, "'You can be anything you want,' somewhat negates and denies what and who they already are, placing them on a treadmill of continually becoming something beyond their immediate selves" (p. 14).

Longitudinal studies of National Merit Scholars provide important evidence for post-high school career development problems related to multipotentiality. A study of 3,089 National Merit Scholars investigated scholastic attainment, educational aspirations, stability of career choice, and clarity of long-range goals (Watley & Kaplan, 1970). Half of the scholars had changed careers once, and many were contemplating still another career. In a follow-up study of the career progress of National Merit Scholar gifted students (1,014 men and 368 women) 8 years after graduation, it was found that precollege plans did not predict vocational and educational decisions (Watley, 1969).

In a study by Fox (1978), gifted boys and girls who took the Strong-Campbell Interest Inventory were compared with a nongifted group of boys and girls. Gifted students scored higher on basic interest scales of writing, mathematics, science, public speaking, and medical science. Gifted girls did not score lower on any interest scale than nongifted girls, and gifted boys scored lower than nongifted boys only on the adventure scale, a measure of immaturity rather than career interests. Gifted students are more interested in intellectual career areas, but not less interested in social, artistic, and conventional career areas than students of average ability. In short, both gifted boys and girls are at least moderately interested in any and all intellectually oriented career areas.

The idea that vocational indecision and vacillation due to multipotentiality may lead to difficulties in adjustment is supported by a longitudinal study by Martins and Pulvino (1975) of "consistent" and "inconsistent" superior students, with consistent defined as having a career similar to the one selected as a goal at graduation. In 1973, the authors collected information on the current employment and vocational adjustment of a group of 86 subjects who had graduated in 1963 from high school and who had participated in the Wisconsin Guidance Laboratory for Superior Students. Consistent and inconsistent subjects were found to differ significantly on self-control, total vocational adjustment, and job status. It seems that those in the consistent gifted group were better able to plan and move toward an occupational goal, and were more satisfied with that goal and achieved higher-status jobs. The inconsistent group, in switching their preferred occupational area one or more times, may have lost the time and planning needed to be as satisfied and successful as their more vocationally consistent peers. Inconsistency of vocational interests at one time, or over a period of time, may be an indication of possible difficulties with multipotentiality.

In summary, it seems that multipotentiality emerges in elementary school and high school as a diversity of abilities, achievements, and interests evidenced by tests and school activities; that multipotential students delay and vacillate among course-taking options and college majors; and that poor career decisions may result in career dissatisfaction in later life.

Too often, multipotential students make misinformed, misguided, or just plain wrong career choices. Today's gifted students make career choices based on conformity with peers, money-making potential, and pragmatism, like the rest of their generation (Astin, Green, & Korn, 1988). Unfortunately, the decisions they make are often not related to interests, needs, strongly held values, or even finely developed talent. The study cited in chapter 4 about the college major and career choices of the upper 10th, 5th, and 1st percentile scorers on ACT composites (Kerr & Colangelo, 1988) and the study of the choices of those students who scored perfectly on at least one scale of the ACT (English, Math, Social Studies, Natural Science) (Colangelo & Kerr, 1990), showed that the majority of the gifted have narrowed their career choices to business, engineering, pre-med, pre-law, and communications. Although perfect scorers had extraordinary abilities in English, math, science, and social studies, only a small fraction were interested in majors in those areas. It is difficult to achieve a perfect score on any of these scales without unusual amounts of extracurricular reading and home study. Yet, these young people, who may value the study of the liberal arts and sciences above all other activities, seem to be discouraged about actually pursuing careers in these areas.

In the absence of information about themselves—that is, how their talents and personalities compare with others', or information about the world of work—it is no wonder that gifted students choose "safe" academic majors. It is sad, though, that students who most value and need cognitive challenge ignore many college majors and career choices that offer the greatest possibility of intellectual stimulation.

## Characteristics of Multipotential Students*

Elementary School

1. Difficulty with making a choice when given an opportunity to choose a topic or project from among many options.
2. Multiple hobbies with only brief periods of enthusiasm.
3. Difficulty in finishing up and following through on tasks, even those that are enjoyable.
4. Excellent performance in many or all school subjects.

Junior High

1. Continued difficulty with decision making.
2. Continued difficulty with follow-through.
3. Continued excellence in many or all school subjects.

---

\* Adapted from Kerr, B. A. (1990). Career Planning for Gifted and Talented Youth. In Berger, S., *Flyer Files on Gifted Students*. Reston, VA: ERIC Clearinghouse on Handicapped and Gifted Children.

4. Multiple social and recreational activities with no clear preferences.
5. "Scheduled up" week with few free periods.

Senior High

1. Decision-making problems generalize to academic and career decisions.
2. Overly packed class schedule with maximum number of courses.
3. Extraordinary diversity of participation in school activities such as athletics, social club, music, newspaper, plays, and departmental clubs.
4. Chosen and appointed as leader of a wide variety of groups in school, religious activities, and community organizations.
5. High marks in most or all courses taken.
6. "High flat" vocational interest test profiles, showing interests and similarities to an unusually large number of occupations.
7. Occasional signs of stress and exhaustion: absences, frequent or chronic illnesses, periods of depression and anxiety, particularly during busiest times.
8. Delay or vacillation about college planning and decision making.

College

1. Multiple academic majors.
2. Three or more changes of college major.
3. Continued intense participation in extracurricular activities.
4. Continued outstanding academic performance.
5. Concern and worry over choice of a career.
6. Hasty, arbitrary, or "going along with the crowd" career choice.

Adulthood

1. Multiple jobs in short time period.
2. Excellent performance in most jobs.
3. General feeling of "lack of fit" in most jobs.
4. Feelings of alienation, purposelessness, depression, and apathy despite high performance and excellent evaluations.
5. Periods of unemployment and underemployment.
6. Pattern of falling behind same-age peers in career progress and sometimes in social development (marriage, family, community involvement).

## Early Emergence

This characteristic of the career development of some gifted students is usually not a concern for individual students, but is often the source of misunderstanding and concern for parents, counselors, and society at large. "Early emergers" (Marshall, 1981) are children who have an extremely focused career interest from a very early age. The example given in the Prologue of Mike, the gifted student with a passion for understanding Einstein's work, is typical of an early emerger. Because a passion for an idea and an early commitment to a career area are actually common childhood characteristics of eminent individuals in a wide variety of professions (Bloom, 1985; Kerr, 1985), early emergence should not be thought of as a "problem" of career development so much as an opportunity that may be acted upon, neglected, or unfortunately, sometimes, destroyed. Acting upon early emergence means noticing an unusually strong talent or enthusiasm, providing training in skills necessary to exercise that talent, providing resources, and keeping an open mind about the future of the talent or interest. Bloom (1985) gave many examples from case studies of how parents, teachers, and mentors all focused energy upon early emergers who became outstanding performers, athletes, and scholars.

Neglecting early emergence means not noticing the talent or interest at all or failing to provide education and resources. Counselors and teachers need to be alert to the appearance of unusual talent and interests not only in traditional academic areas, but also in such areas as inventiveness and leadership. They should also be aware that a child's passion and brilliance at such recreational activities as Nintendo, Dungeons and Dragons, or skateboarding may be a sign of early emerging spatial-visual genius, verbal creativity, and athletic excellence, respectively. Ignoring these abilities because they emerge in play may be costly to the student's career development.

Destroying the early emerger's passion may not be easy, but it is done by belittling the talent or interest ("Who cares about someone who doodles and draws all the time instead of listening?" "So what makes you think you will ever be able to get a job as an anthropologist?"). It can also be done by insisting on "well-roundedness." Although the concept of the "well-rounded" person is deeply embedded in American educational tradition, research does not support the notion that eminent adults are knowledgeable in all fields or competent in all skills. Too often teachers and parents mistake a specialized interest as evidence of imbalance or poor adjustment when there is no basis for this evaluation. Sometimes parents or schools actively disallow needed training (e.g., refusing to allow a mathematically precocious child to accelerate in math), causing a talent to wither. Finally, overly enthusiastic encouragement and pressure may also remove the intrinsic pleasure the child feels in the interest or talent area. When a child's first, tentative explorations of piano playing show precocious ability, too intense a practice schedule and concentrated parental focus may kill the child's natural desire to play well.

## Characteristics of Early Emergers*

Elementary

1. Avid interest in only one school subject or activity with only general liking for other subjects and activities.
2. Uneven talent development, with extraordinary talent in one area and average or above-average performance in others (may be mistakenly labeled as "underachiever").
3. Desire to write most papers or choose most subjects in the area of interest.
4. Early career fantasies about success and fame in the area of interest.

Junior High

1. Continued highly focused interests.
2. Strong desire for advanced training in area of talent and interest.
3. Slow development of adolescent social interests because of commitment to work in talent area or because of rejection by others.
4. High performance in talent area, but not necessarily in others.

Senior High

1. Strongly developed identity in talent area, i.e., "the computer whiz," "the artist," or "the fix-it person."

---

* Adapted from Kerr, B. A. (1990). Career Planning for Gifted and Talented Youth. In Berger, S., *Flyer Files on Gifted Students*. Reston, VA: ERIC Clearinghouse on Handicapped and Gifted Children.

2. Desire for help with planning a career in area of interest.
3. Desire to test skill in competition with or in concert with peers in the talent area.
4. Continued high performance in talent area, with possible neglect of other school subjects or social activities.

College/Young Adulthood

1. Early choice of career or major.
2. Desire for completion of training period in order to "get on with work."
3. Seeking of mentors in area of interest.
4. Continued intense focus.
5. Possible neglect of social and extracurricular activities.

Adulthood

1. Continued intense focus.
2. Desire for eminence or excellence in talent area.
3. Possible foregoing or delay of other aspects of adult development such as marriage, nurturing of younger generation, social and community involvement, and personal development.

## Career Education and Guidance

It should be clear from the foregoing sections that career interventions need to begin very early for gifted and talented students. This does not mean that bright students should be pressured into making early career choices. Instead, career education should be infused into the curriculum and career guidance strategies added to the curriculum to help gifted students progress through the stages of fantasy, exploration, crystallization, and commitment to a career. Career education and guidance for gifted students need to take into account not only their special career development needs, but also their preferences for intellectually challenging materials and methods. Finally, career education and guidance need to be based on the discovery of a vocation or purpose rather than the search for a job. Teaching students how to "package" themselves via resumes and interviewing skills should be deemphasized in favor of teaching students the importance of career development as a search for meaning.

The author has written two career education guides for gifted students, *Career Education for Gifted and Talented* (Kerr, 1982) and *Career Planning for Gifted and Talented Youth* (Kerr, 1990). The following strategies are adapted from these guides.

## Interventions for Multipotentiality*

Elementary

1. Provide realistic exposure to world of work. Encourage parents to share information about their work; tour work places of parents; tour work places of friends of parents and teachers who are professionals (such as physicians, engineers, college professors, and free-lance artists).
2. Encourage career fantasies through dress-up and plays. Keep boxes of costumes and props at home, in the classroom, in the elementary counselor's office.
3. Encourage focus on activities that require goal setting and follow-through (class projects, scout badges).
4. Use biographies of eminent people as primary career education material. Facilitate book discussion groups centered around the lives of eminent people in science, the arts, education, government, and entertainment.
5. Help teachers and parents evaluate skills, talents, and interests carefully in order to help the child understand possible areas of greatest interest.

Junior High

1. Help junior high students discuss meaning and value of work.
2. Discuss family and community values pertaining to work.
3. Keep a referral list of light volunteer work in several areas of interest.
4. Provide several "shadowing" experiences in which the student spends the day with an adult working in areas of greatest interest.

---

* Adapted from Kerr, B. A. (1990). Career Planning for Gifted and Talented Youth. In Berger, S., *Flyer Files on Gifted Students*. Reston, VA: ERIC Clearinghouse on Handicapped and Gifted Children.

5. Discourage overinvolvement in social and recreational activities for the sake of involvement; help students set priorities and decide on a few extracurricular involvements.

Senior High

1. Provide appropriate vocational testing for interests, personality characteristics, and values.
2. Arrange visits to college and university classes in a few areas of interest.
3. Encourage more extensive volunteer work.
4. List possibilities of paid internships with professionals.
5. Help student plan a solid curriculum of coursework in order to insure against inadequate preparation for a later career choice.
6. Provide value-based guidance emphasizing choosing a career that fulfills deeply held values.
7. Discourage conformist, stereotyped career choices.

College and Young Adulthood

1. Provide career counseling that includes assessment of interests, needs, and values.
2. Encourage enrollment in career planning class.
3. Encourage careful course selection.
4. Help student seek a mentor.
5. Help student engage in long-term goal setting and planning for postsecondary training.

## Interventions for Early Emergers

Elementary

1. Help to select measures and strategies for early identification of unusual talents or areas of precocity.
2. Consult with experts on the nature and nurture of particular gifts or talents.
3. Consult with teachers and administrators on ways of nurturing the talent or gift.
4. Encourage fantasies through reading bibliographies and role playing work.

5. Provide opportunities to learn about eminent people in the talent area (attend a concert featuring a famous musician; visit an inventor's workshop in the area; attend a math professor's class).
6. Help teachers design ways of relating other, necessary basic skills to area of interest.
7. Provide lists and guides to opportunities to socialize with children with similar, intense interests through such activities as music camps, computer camps, Junior Great Books.
8. Help parents and teachers strike a careful balance between encouragement and laissez-faire. Provide support for the strong interest along with freedom to change direction. Don't become so invested in the child's talent or interests that you don't notice that the child has changed interests. (Early emergers most often change to a closely related interest; that is, they switch musical instruments or transfer an interest in math to an interest in theoretical physics).

Junior High

1. Provide support and encouragement during the intensive training that often begins at this point.
2. Encourage students to seek plenty of alone time.
3. Provide opportunities for job "shadowing" (following a professional throughout the working day) in area of interest.
4. Provide opportunities for light volunteer work in area of interest.
5. Caution parents to avoid pressuring the student into social activities.

Senior High

1. Continue support, encouragement, and alone time.
2. Provide opportunities for internships and work experiences in areas of interest (internship or archaeological dig; camp counselor at fine arts camp; coaching younger people in musical or athletic skill).
3. Provide career guidance referrals to a guidance professional *who is familiar with the talent area* or to a professional in that field.
4. Help the student make a detailed plan of training and education leading toward the chosen career goal, including financial arrangements.
5. Encourage the student to explore higher education or postsecondary training early and thoroughly, with contacts and visits.

6. Help the student establish a relationship with a mentor in the area of interest. Early emergers are often better off in less prestigious institutions where they have access to an enthusiastic mentor than in an Ivy League or high-status institution where they do not.

College and Young Adulthood

1. Help provide support for extended education and training.
2. Encourage the development of knowledge of ''career ladders'' in the area of interest (auditions, gallery shows, inventors' conventions, etc.).
3. Encourage a continuing relationship with a career counseling or guidance professional for support in decision making and problem solving.

## The Guidance Laboratory Approach as a Counseling Strategy

The guidance laboratory is a collection of research-based counseling interventions designed to prevent career-related problems (Kerr & Ghrist-Priebe, 1988). For multipotential students, the guidance laboratory offers informational assessment and counseling that culminates in commitment to a specific career goal. For the student who has stereotyped or unconsidered career choices, the guidance laboratory provides the challenge to explore careers that are likely to actualize the student's values as well as to explore the creative synthesis of two or more career areas (e.g., arts management; music therapy; teaching architecture). For the student who has deficits in course preparation, the guidance laboratory offers specific information about requirements for entry into college majors and careers.

The intervention is a 1-day career counseling workshop in which students participate in gender-balanced groups of 8 to 12. As soon as the students arrive, introductions are made, and the students are informed of the day's schedule. Next, all students complete the Self-Directed Search (Holland, 1974) or the Vocational Preference Inventory (Holland, 1985); the Edwards Personal Preference Schedule (EPPS) (Edwards, 1959) or the Personality Research Form (Jackson, 1974); the Rokeach Values Survey (Rokeach, 1982); and a short questionnaire about academic and extracurricular activities. Afterward, students are allowed to select any part of the university to visit (e.g., the computer center or library) and are taken there by a student host. Next, they select and attend a university class related to their area of career interest. After the class visits, students have lunch with guidance laboratory counselors who discuss the morning's experiences, the students' school activities, and future plans in pairs and triads. In the afternoon, students participate in individual and group counseling sessions.

All individual counseling sessions are 50 minutes long. In these sessions, the counselors follow a structured interview schedule designed to (a) clarify interests, needs, and values; (b) indicate understanding of student concerns; (c) encourage practice in goal setting; and (d) influence students to make career decisions based on their interests, needs, and values. To accomplish the first objective, the counselors interpret the results of the assessment instruments, helping the client to synthesize this information. The counselors demonstrate, on the basis of the test results, how each client is unique or special. The following is an example of such an interpretation:

> You have a Holland code IES—a very rare code because it combines two very different sets of personality characteristics, the Investigative personality's love of ideas, science, and analysis and the Enterprising personality's interests in selling and persuading. In addition, the "S" for Social in your code and your EPPS scores on Need for Affiliation (90th percentile) and need for Exhibition (95th percentile!) show that you have a special affinity for people and being out in front of people. I'll bet Carl Sagan has a profile like this—and I'll bet that you, too, would be very good at selling scientific ideas to the public. Your highest values, Knowledge and Friendship, certainly seem to fit; what do you think?

To encourage the practice of goal setting, counselors present clients with a goal-setting sheet. In this exercise, they suggest that clients choose any future goal—perhaps based on the test interpretation discussion—and describe, on the goal-setting sheet, the steps necessary to take this week, this month, this year, and thereafter to attain the goal.

The counselors help clients to focus by giving information and encouragement. Finally, they help clients to feel understood and supported by using verbal following and open-ended questions throughout the interview. Also, they demonstrate their support by showing curiosity rather than ignorance when their clients discuss topics such as science fiction or violin concertos, about which the counselors might know very little.

All students also participate in a group life planning session with a counselor and four to seven students. The objectives of this session are to focus on specific aspects of the students' desired future life-styles and to identify barriers as well as possibilities in attaining those life-styles. To accomplish these objectives, the counselor leads the students in a "Perfect Future Day" fantasy (Zunker, 1983) in which students imagine an entire working day 10 years in their own future. After the fantasy, students are led in a discussion of possibilities and barriers, with the counselor encouraging high aspirations and giving information when necessary.

The workshop ends with a short lecture reiterating the purposes of the workshop and encouraging continued career decision making. Evaluations of the workshop are distributed, and students are given an opportunity to request additional counseling anonymously. Additional materials for the guidance laboratory are included in the Resources section.

The guidance laboratory approach has been found to be effective in stimulating gifted students to begin the process of career exploration. Students who have attended the guidance laboratory are more likely to discuss their career plans with parents, teachers, and counselors and to have followed up on career ideas than students who have not attended (Kerr & Ghrist-Priebe, 1988). Gifted girls who attend the guidance laboratory tend to raise their career aspirations, and gifted boys maintain their high career aspirations (Kerr, 1983). Finally, a variant of the guidance laboratory approach, when applied to college students, seems to be effective in enhancing gifted students' sense of purpose and identity (Kerr, 1990).

Therefore, counselors should consider the possibility of arranging a partnership with the counseling or career center of a nearby college or university for the purpose of career guidance for gifted students. Guidance laboratories are that rare case in which a well-planned, 1-day experience can have a powerful and lasting effect on the fulfillment of bright students' career potential.

## Summary

Lack of appropriate career guidance can prevent gifted students from achieving their full potential. Gifted students have unique career development needs. Multipotential gifted students do many things well and have a wide variety of interests; they often need help with focusing on a limited number of activities and with goal setting. Early emergers need help in coping with their precocious passions; counselors need to support them in the face of discouragement. Values-based interventions may be particularly helpful to gifted students who are seeking meaning and purpose as well as a career.

## References

Astin, A., Green, K. C., & Korn, W. S. (1988). *The American freshman: Twenty year trends*. Los Angeles: Higher Education Research Institute.

Bloom, B. S. (1985). *Developing talent in young people*. New York: Ballantine Books.

Colangelo, N., & Kerr, B. A. (1990). Extreme academic talent: Profiles of perfect scorers. *Journal of Educational Psychology, 82,* 404–409.

Colangelo, N., & Zaffrann, R. A. (1979). *New voices in counseling the gifted.* Dubuque, IA: Kendall-Hunt.

Cox, J., Daniel, N., & Boston, B. O. (1985). *Educating able learners: Programs and promising practices*. Austin, TX: University of Austin Press.

Edwards, A. L. (1983). *Edwards Personal Preference Schedule*. New York: Psychological Corporation.

Fox, L. H. (1978). Interest correlates to differential achievement of gifted students in mathematics. *Journal for the Education of the Gifted, 1,* 24–36.

Frederickson, R. H., & Rothney, J. W. M. (1972). *Recognizing and assisting multipotential youth*. Columbus, OH: Merrill.

Holland, J. (1974). *Self-Directed Search*. Palo Alto, CA: Consulting Psychologists Press.

Holland, J. (1985). *The Vocational Preference Inventory*. Odessa, FL: Psychological Assessment Resources.

Hollingworth, L. S. (1926). *Gifted children: Their nature and nurture*. New York: Macmillan.

Jackson, D. N. (1974). *The Personality Research Form*. Odessa, FL: Psychological Assessment Resources.

Kaufmann, F. (1981). The 1964–1968 Presidential Scholars: A follow-up study. *Exceptional Children, 48,* 2.

Kerr, B. A. (1981). Career education strategies for gifted and talented. *Journal of Career Education, 7,* 318–325. Reprinted in Chronical Guidance Professional Series, p. 994, 1982.

Kerr, B. A. (1982). *Career education for the gifted and talented*. Columbus, OH: ERIC Clearinghouse on Adult, Career and Vocational Education.

Kerr, B. A. (1983). Raising aspirations of gifted girls. *Vocational Guidance Quarterly, 32*, 37–44.

Kerr, B. A. (1985). *Smart girls, gifted women.* Columbus, OH: Ohio Psychology.

Kerr, B. A. (1990). Career planning for gifted and talented youth. In Berger, S. *Flyer files on gifted students.* Reston, VA: ERIC Clearinghouse on Handicapped and Gifted Children.

Kerr, B. A., & Colangelo, N. (1988). The college plans of academically talented students. *Journal of Counseling and Development, 67*(1), 42–49.

Kerr, B. A., & Ghrist-Priebe, S. (1988). Intervention for multipotentiality. *Journal of Counseling and Development, 66*(8), 366–370.

Marshall, B. C. (1981). Career decision-making patterns of gifted and talented adolescents. *Journal of Career Education, 7*, 305–310.

Perrone, P., Karshner, W., & Male, R. (1979). *The career development needs of talented students.* University of Wisconsin (ERIC No. ED 185 731).

Rokeach, M. (1982). *Rokeach Values Inventory.* Sunnyvale, CA: Halgren Press.

Roper, C. J., & Berry, K. (1986). College career centers: Reaching out to the gifted and talented. *Journal of Career Development, 13*(1), 26–30.

Sanborn, M. P. (1979). Career development: Problems of gifted and talented students. In N. Colangelo & R. Zaffrann (Eds.), *New voices in counseling the gifted* (pp. 186–196). Dubuque, IA: Kendall-Hunt.

Terman, L. M., & Oden, M. H. (1935). The promise of youth. *Genetic studies of genius*, Vol. 3. Stanford: Stanford University Press.

Terman, L. M., & Oden, M. H. (1947). The gifted child grows up. *Genetic studies of genius*, Vol. 4. Stanford: Stanford University Press.

Watley, D. J. (1969). *Stability of career choices of talented youth.* Evanston, IL: National Merit Scholar Corporation.

Watley, D. J., & Kaplan, R. (1970). *Merit scholars and the fulfillment of promise.* Evanston, IL: National Merit Scholar Corporation.

Zunker, A. (1983). *Career counseling.* Monterey, CA: Brooks-Cole.

# 6

# Counseling Gifted and Talented Girls

Those who work with gifted girls are often frustrated by their failure to live up to the expectations of their youth. Guidance counselors often observe that gifted young women seem gradually to disengage themselves from goal setting throughout adolescence. Girls who at the beginning of junior high have ambitious dreams often have forgotten those dreams by the end of junior high and seem to have only the most stereotypic notions of what they want to do with the rest of their lives (Kerr, 1985).

It is often difficult for counselors to pinpoint exactly what seems to be holding bright girls back. What are the barriers to gifted girls' achievement? How do we overcome those barriers? It is clear that the problem of finding the reason that gifted girls don't live up to their potential is not a straightforward task at all. This is because, as we have seen in chapter 1 on identification, our ideas about what constitutes intelligence are changing; our values as a society about the role of women are changing; and finally, every year gifted girls themselves undergo a flux in their attitudes and values.

New concepts of intelligence such as Sternberg's information processing approach (Sternberg & Davidson, 1986) and Gardner's (1983) theory of multiple intelligences are challenging the notion of the unitary IQ as the only way of measuring intellectual performance. However, most of the newer theories of intelligence do not speak to the problem of female giftedness. These theories have little or nothing to say about gender. Therefore, we again have the problem that we have had with more traditional theories of intelligence: We don't understand how these theories apply to gifted girls. Nevertheless, counselors need to make decisions based on the best available information, and with an eye to broadening the concept of intelligence.

Our society is also changing its attitudes toward gifted girls. Value conflicts today pervade society, education, and research. Although the majority of American women now work outside the home, our society has a deep ambivalence about this change. Stories about the dangers of becoming superwomen, criticisms about the effects of child care rather than mother care, and a great deal of interest in sex differences and abilities seem to be the symptoms of this ambivalence. Counselors cannot avoid the discussion of values; they must understand clearly their own values and respect those held by the gifted girls they counsel.

There are also value conflicts within the professions of psychology and education about women's roles. Many researchers cannot agree on how to study women's abilities, and many feminist researchers claim that women's achievement should not be measured by the same scales as male achievement. Gilligan's (1982) proposal that women experience a different process of moral development than do men has provided a base for these ideas. Although counselors may find themselves caught in value conflicts in the profession, they still must find practical solutions to help gifted girls make the choices that will most likely lead to the fulfillment of their potential.

Finally, gifted girls themselves are changing. In the last 10 years extraordinary changes have occurred in gifted girls' career aspirations and academic achievement. Where studies in the early 1980s showed that gifted young women often had lower aspirations than gifted young men (Kerr, 1983), currently young women are choosing some professional careers in almost equal proportions as are young men (Kerr & Colangelo, 1988).

Parents' attitudes toward their gifted daughters are also changing. Many parents are determined that their daughters will succeed in achieving their dreams and goals. A study by Jacobs and Eccles (1985) found that fathers' attitudes toward their daughters' mathematical abilities actually improved after reading media reports about studies of gender differences favoring boys in mathematics. Changes that are occurring in the attitudes of gifted girls and in the attitudes of their parents mean that special guidance strategies for gifted girls and young women will be particularly needed and appreciated. The next sections will review what is known about gifted girls and gifted female adolescents and present suggestions for guidance and counseling.

## Gifted Girls

Girls often show their giftedness at an earlier age than boys (Silverman, 1986). In addition, high-IQ girls tend to be taller, stronger, and healthier than girls of average IQ. In the moderately gifted range, gifted girls tend to be very well adjusted, whether this social adjustment is measured in terms of social knowledge (Terman & Oden, 1935), perceived self-confidence (Chan, 1988), or absence of behavioral impairments on behavior rating scales (Ludwig & Cullinan, 1984). Gifted girls seem to be very free of childhood adjustment disorders. However, highly gifted girls may experience more adjustment problems (Kerr, 1985). In general, the highest-IQ children suffer more adjustment problems, simply as a result of being so very deviant from the norm. Gifted girls seem to experience this deviance even more profoundly.

Throughout childhood gifted girls are more similar to gifted boys than they are to average girls in their interests, attitudes, and aspirations. Gifted girls like many of the same play activities that gifted boys enjoy, such as outdoor activities, adventures, sports, and problem solving. However, they may also have feminine interests. They may enjoy dolls and girls' magazines; but they may play with girls' toys in more creative or exploratory ways. It is also common for gifted girls to spend a great deal of time alone and to enjoy this alone time (Kerr, 1985).

Although most girls have fairly stereotyped career interests by second grade, gifted girls may have career interests more like those of gifted boys. Young gifted girls often have adventurous aspirations. They want to be great writers, paleontologists, astronauts, or diplomats. Gifted girls are also similar to gifted boys in their academic interests; however, they tend to outperform gifted boys throughout school, attaining higher grades in most school subjects. Gifted girls also outperform gifted boys on achievement tests throughout elementary school.

## Adolescent Gifted Girls

With adolescence come major changes in gifted girls' attitudes toward their career goals, in their intellectual and social interests, and in their actual achievement. Whereas once these changes were dramatic, in the last 10 years they have become more subtle. Adolescent gifted girls seem to be aware that they are expected to maintain high career aspirations and high academic achievement. Nevertheless, there is often a marked decline in their involvement with their former academic goals or an indifference to their own stated career goals.

## Declining Academic Achievement in Adolescence

Several studies show that at the highest level of achievement on college admissions tests, gifted girls score lower than gifted boys. On ACT exams, taken during the senior year of high school, 61% of students scoring above the 95th percentile on the composite score are male, and 72% of students scoring in the 99th percentile on the composite score are also male (Kerr & Colangelo, 1988). Men also outperform women on three of the four subtests at the highest levels. Three times as many men achieve perfect scores in math as do women; five times as many men get perfect natural sciences scores as do women; and two and one half times as many men achieve perfect social studies scores as do women. Only on the English subtests do women outperform men (Colangelo & Kerr, 1990).

A study by Laing, Engen, and Maxey (1987) shows that much of the variance in ACT scores can be accounted for by course taking. It seems likely that the lower scores for women on the ACT are strongly related to course taking. Gifted adolescent girls apparently take fewer and less challenging math and science courses than do boys. In addition, they take less challenging social studies courses. As a result, gifted adolescent girls are less prepared than are gifted boys for the more rigorous colleges.

## Sex Differences in Mathematics

Sex differences in mathematical ability have also been found in a more select group of gifted boys and girls who participated in the Talent Search program (Benbow & Stanley, 1984). These extreme sex differences favoring boys were puzzling in that the seventh graders had taken very similar courses. This study continues to be a source of controversy. Many scholars emphasize that girls and boys within the same classroom may be receiving differential treatment (Sadker & Sadker, 1984); other scholars suggest that the boys' higher scores on the SAT mathematical exam represent higher levels of inherent mathematical reasoning ability (Benbow & Stanley, 1984).

Whatever the actual source of sex differences in math achievement, counselors should keep in mind several facts when guiding gifted girls. First of all, math differences that have been observed in junior high students have been observed only at the very highest level of ability. Therefore, at moderately high levels of ability boys and girls perform similarly. Counselors should also remember that the highest level of mathematical ability required by even the most rigorous, math-related professions is well within the reach of gifted girls. Finally, it is likely that the differences in math ability observed by teachers and counselors are due to factors within our control. Equitable teaching in the classrooms, high expectations of girls, and guidance into appropriate course taking can go a long way toward ensuring that gifted girls will be high math achievers (Sadker & Sadker, 1985).

## Aspirations of the Gifted Adolescent Girl

Until recently counselors have observed that gifted girls tended to lower their career aspirations between junior high and the beginning of college. At one time, only highly gifted girls such as the top 1% of National Merit Scholars usually maintained high career aspirations throughout adolescence (Kaufmann, 1981). Now, however, most gifted adolescent girls are naming college majors that are nontraditional for women. Among girls scoring in the 95th percentile and above on ACT, about as many girls as boys choose majors in pre-medicine, pre-law, and even mathematics (Kerr & Colangelo, 1988).

Most recent studies do show that gifted adolescent girls are now aiming high when they are asked to name their career goals. However, few studies of gifted adolescent girls go beyond eliciting career choice. Many counselors have observed at the Counseling Laboratory for Talent Development at The University of Iowa that beyond being able to name a career goal, many bright young women seem to be uncertain and confused about how to reach that goal or what the goal means. Apparently, gifted adolescent girls have learned to name ambitious career goals but have not considered what these goals mean to their lives.

Counselors at the Counseling Laboratory have also observed that gifted girls now seem to be reluctant to discuss conflicts they feel between career and family. Perhaps this is because it is simply assumed that women will both work and have a family. Gifted girls also may want to avoid discussing such an anxiety-laden topic. Nevertheless, it is clear that these conflicts do exist and that bright young women need an opportunity to discuss their fears or concerns openly.

## Psychological Adjustment of Gifted Girls

Most gifted girls, like gifted boys, are well adjusted. Most moderately gifted girls receive high scores on personality inventories in psychological characteristics associated with good mental health and adjustment. However, there do seem to be some critical periods during the development of a gifted adolescent girl when increases in social anxiety may occur. In one study, Groth (1969) showed an abrupt psychological shift at age 14 from wishes and needs related to achievement to wishes related to love and belonging. The girls in this study had apparently dropped their dreams of success in favor of dreams of popularity. Current studies have also shown increases in social anxiety during adolescence. For instance, Kelly and Colangelo (1984) found that gifted girls were not superior to average girls in academic and social self-concept although gifted boys were superior to average boys in these characteristics. Similarly, Kerr, Colangelo, and Gaeth (1988) found that gifted girls were very concerned about the impact of their giftedness on the attitudes of others. Although gifted boys were likely to see some social advantages to being gifted, gifted girls saw fewer advantages.

Constance Hollinger and Elise Fleming have done some of the most important work in the area of gifted girls' self-esteem and adjustment. These researchers believe that social self-esteem (Hollinger, 1983) is critical to the realization of potential in gifted girls. Girls with high social self-esteem will show high "instrumentality" and high "expressiveness." Instrumentality is the ability to act effectively and make decisions independently. Expressiveness is the ability to be responsive and caring.

Instrumentality seems to be more important to high self-esteem than expressiveness, although expressiveness is also important. Social self-esteem seems to help girls overcome fears of social rejection and helps to build self-confidence. Hollinger and Fleming (1984) found that gifted girls' self-perceptions of instrumentality were strongly related to the occupational confidence and the satisfaction with life that they felt 3½ years after graduation. Counselors need to discover ways to develop instrumentality in gifted girls and also to maintain the expressive characteristics that are a part of most gifted girls' personality.

Counselors also need to be aware that too much emphasis may be placed on gifted girls' good social adjustment. In fact, good social adjustment is not necessarily a predictor of eminence. Kaufmann (1981) found that among Presidential Scholars many girls were perceived as loners; yet these young women went on to accomplishments at least equal to those of their male peers. Kerr (1985) found that although eminent women often had unhappy adolescences, they were able to overcome feelings of rejection and were able to develop independence. Therefore, although it is important that counselors nurture instrumentality and expressiveness in order to build self-esteem and confidence, it is not necessary for counselors to be overly concerned about a gifted girl's lack of popularity or desire for solitude.

## How Counselors Can Help Gifted Girls

Counselors can assist in the personal and career development of gifted girls beginning in elementary school and continuing throughout adulthood. They can help both as consultants to teachers and parents and as direct counselors and advisors to gifted girls. Several ways in which counselors can serve as consultants include assisting in identification of the gifted and talented; helping teachers achieve equity in the classroom; and serving as career education consultants. Ways in which counselors can have individual impact on gifted girls include advisement for challenging course taking; building social self-esteem; helping girls overcome perceived barriers; and assisting in the process of falling in love with an idea.

## Identification

Counselors may serve as assistants in the identification process of the gifted and talented as was described in chapter 1 on identification. It is important during this process that counselors help identification teams to become aware of special issues affecting the identification of giftedness in girls. Because gifted girls are more likely to show developmental advancement than gifted boys and are more likely to be ready for kindergarten earlier than gifted boys, identification procedures for giftedness should begin early with gifted girls (Silverman, 1986; Callahan, 1979). Although intelligence tests such as the Stanford-Binet, the WISC-R, and the Kaufman ABC have been used with very young children, they are not often reliable measures of giftedness before 9 years of age. Therefore, in order to ensure the appropriate placement of very young gifted girls, it is often necessary to combine evidence from intelligence tests with signs of school readiness, such as advanced vocabulary, precocious reading, precocious math skills, and an eagerness for school social activities. Particularly in school districts where "proof" of giftedness is required, it may be necessary to test girls with one of these three identification instruments and to prepare detailed behavior descriptions.

Counselors need to serve as consultants for identification programs at all levels to ensure equity in selection procedures. For instance, counselors can ensure that tests used for admission to gifted education programs have minimal sex bias. Tests that emphasize content more familiar to boys than girls are biased tests. Items clearly biased toward boys may be items concerning mechanics, sports, careers, and other extraneous content that has been traditionally masculine. Even items that feature more diagrams may be biased in favor of boys (Doolittle & Cleary, 1987). These items reflect boys' reading and daily experiences rather than the experiences of girls in our society. Achievement tests with a heavier weighting of math and science items than language-related items will also be biased against girls, especially in the higher grades. Intelligence tests that emphasize spatial-visual activities may also select fewer girls, possibly because girls receive much less practice than boys at spatial-visual tasks such as assembly and building of toys.

In junior high it may become important to use differential cutoffs when identification strategies clearly yield more boys than girls. This has been a common practice in Talent Search programs where the SAT-M identifies more boys than girls for accelerated math programs. This does not mean that accelerated math classes will be harder for girls with lower scores. It is very likely that a girl scoring 510 on SAT-M will perform as well in an accelerated mathematics class as a boy scoring 530. Because the tests predict differently for boys and girls, lower scores for girls may predict the same degree of success. A multidimensional approach to identification may also ensure that girls with potential for high academic achievement are identified (Fleming & Hollinger, 1979). Multidimensional approaches take into account such characteristics as creativity and leadership. This technique is particularly useful for selecting minority girls who have been brought up in a traditional fashion or rural girls who may not have been exposed to many opportunities for girls and women. It is likely that girls who have not had challenging coursework will be identified through creativity and leadership techniques.

Counselors should bear in mind that no objective measures have actually been shown to be associated with accomplishment of gifted women as adults. Tests of intellectual aptitude and achievement can only be used to predict academic performance. But the counselor must understand that many powerful nonacademic factors may determine the progress a gifted girl makes toward achieving her goals.

## Assisting Teachers in Achieving Equity in the Classroom

There is undeniable evidence that boys receive more attention from teachers and higher quality instruction than do girls throughout their education (Sadker & Sadker, 1985). Teachers respond more often to boys than to girls in class and boys are more frequently rewarded for calling out answers, whereas girls are rewarded for being quiet and cooperative. Boys also receive more informative responses from teachers; teachers are more likely to give girls bland responses, whereas boys are given praise and criticism. Boys are given much more detailed instructions on how to approach tasks and solve problems, whereas girls are often simply given the right answer. None of this behavior seems to be conscious on the teachers' part because even teachers who strongly support girls' rights to self-development find themselves responding more to boys than to girls. Apparently there is an interaction between the boys' more lively assertion and the teachers' "programming" in differential responding to boys and girls.

On an optimistic note, however, Sadker and Sadker (1985) also found that teachers can learn fairly quickly to overcome sex-biased teaching. Through a series of workshops that involve videotaping their instruction, evaluating their responses to boys and girls, and relearning responding techniques, teachers are able to achieve more equitable teaching in the classroom. Counselors can help teachers to achieve equitable teaching by using Sadker and Sadker's (1985) methods and by suggesting ways in which teachers can call on girls in equal proportions and challenge girls to solve problems for themselves.

Some evidence shows that teachers' attitudes toward gifted girls may be more negative than their attitudes toward girls in general (Solano, 1977). Other studies have shown that female teachers may sometimes be more discouraging of gifted girls' aspirations than are male teachers and that occasionally gifted girls have been discouraged from taking advanced math courses, entering gifted education, and participating in summer opportunities. When counselors discover that girls have been discouraged in any of these ways, it is important that they intervene not only with the girls but also with the teachers.

First, it will often be necessary for the counselor to challenge stereotypes that students and teachers may have of appropriate courses and career goals for girls. Second, it is important that counselors provide positive strategies and suggestions for teachers in creating more equitable classrooms. Third, at all times counselors must provide a model of non-sexist behavior. This means attending to girls as often as boys; being sure that girls have as many opportunities for scholarships and college information as boys; giving girls full informative, challenging responses; rewarding girls' assertiveness; and resisting overhelping girls by solving all their personal, career, or social development problems for them.

## Career Education

Counselors can also serve as career education consultants to the classroom teacher. Most packaged career education approaches are not appropriate for gifted students in general, as explained in chapter 5 on career counseling. This is also true for career education approaches for girls. Many career education approaches designed for average girls, although focusing on nontraditional careers, may overemphasize lower-level careers. Therefore career education for gifted girls must be patterned after career education for gifted students in general.

Career education for gifted girls should incorporate as its primary reading material the biographies of eminent women (Kerr, 1985). Gifted girls will often see themselves in the stories of the lives of eminent women. Biographies provide not only a narrative of the events of the lives of talented women but also show the necessary steps to achieve success in many professional fields. A bibliography for gifted girls appears in the Resources section of this book.

Another important element of career education is the use of models. Role models have been given a great deal of emphasis in career workshops with girls. It can be useful for gifted girls to meet and to discuss careers with women who are successful in science, math, politics, engineering, and other fields where women are rare. However, it is important to be aware of the principles of effective modeling when choosing people who are to speak to or interact with gifted girls. For role modeling to be effective, it is necessary that the girls observe the models being reinforced for their career behavior. Professional women who complain about being overburdened or who stress the difficulties they encountered achieving their goal may have a negative effect on gifted girls.

Gifted girls, hearing of the great struggles that model women have encountered may decide that it is just not worth it to try to attain high goals. Therefore, models should be women who are highly accomplished in their careers, and women who are happy and satisfied with their lives. It is important that role models provide examples of how women can combine career and family successfully. They should clearly come across as lively, capable, and happy with the reward they are receiving for their work and their life-style.

Job shadowing and job tryout also provide an opportunity for gifted girls to experience what particular careers would be like. Job shadowing is spending a day or more working alongside an adult in her or his normal working routines. Again, it is the choice of the mentor with whom the student will gain the work experience that is critical to the success of the program. Gifted girls should be placed for shadowing experiences only with women who can show clearly not only what they do on the job, but what they have done to get there. Like model women, mentors should be contented with their work and life-style and should be able to express that to the girls who are working with them.

Finally, counselors can initiate special programs that may involve teachers, students, and community women. Examples of workshops for gifted girls include career education opportunities in informal and entertaining ways. One of these is the Career Education Workshop developed in Louisville,

Kentucky, by Bonnie Roth of the Creative Learning Institute. These career workshops bring together teachers, members of the local Junior League, and gifted girls to provide a day-long series of activities focusing on gifted girls' future roles. The day's activities include keynote speeches by experts on career development of gifted girls; group activities and discussions focusing on helping girls identify barriers to their goals and ways of overcoming those barriers; and panels of distinguished and accomplished Kentucky women to serve as models.

Another example of a successful career education program is the "Going for your Goals" Conference provided by the Iowa City Community Schools Foundation. This workshop, which was created by a planning committee made up of teachers, community women, and University of Iowa faculty, was also a day-long series of activities. Activities included a perfect future day fantasy, group discussions of roles, and most important, practice in setting specific goals and predicting the steps necessary to attain those goals. Throughout the day girls interacted in small groups led by a model woman.

Finally, one of the most creative examples of career education for gifted girls is the Math/Science Sleepover, which was developed by gifted education coordinator Dexter Schraer and teachers of the gifted in Columbia, Missouri, public schools. The Math/Science Sleepover is an all-night pajama party for gifted girls, teachers, and women mathematicians and scientists. Activities include movies about the lives of well-known women scientists, a pizza party with university women faculty in science and math, group discussions about girls' personal career goals, and a scavenger hunt involving math and science riddles.

Programs like these can serve several functions in that they include information, mentoring, modeling, and problem solving. They can make a great difference in the lives of gifted girls. However, to be most effective, career education for gifted girls should not be based on a one-shot activity. An event such as a workshop or an overnight should be followed by other activities designed to maintain the learning and the commitments that are made.

## Advising Gifted Girls

Although many counselors regret that so much of their time is spent in registration and advisement rather than in personal counseling, it is in the area of advisement that counselors may be able to have the greatest impact on the lives of gifted girls. Gifted girls' course-taking decisions not only affect their junior and high school academic life; they also affect the scores they will achieve on college admissions tests, the types of colleges and universities to which they will be accepted, their success in particular college majors, and their eventual choice of a career.

Too often, even the brightest girls in mathematics are able to persuade their parents, teachers, and counselors that they will not succeed in advanced math and science courses. Those counselors who themselves disliked math and science may feel sympathetic with a gifted girl's fears of failure in these courses. Nevertheless, it is crucial that the counselor not collaborate with the gifted girl's attempts to avoid math and science.

Counselors need to share information with gifted girls about course-taking choices that will help them make appropriate decisions. Some examples of facts gifted girls need to be aware of are:

- The majority of college majors that lead to high status, high salary, and high levels of independence on the job require 4 years of high school mathematics preparation. These careers are not only science-related careers, but also careers in business, journalism, and even in areas such as linguistics, which require computer expertise.
- College admissions officers look more favorably upon those students whose transcripts show that they have completed a rigorous series of courses with a moderately high grade point average than upon those whose transcripts show very high grades in easy courses.
- Most gifted girls who are in the moderate ranges on math and science achievement, such as the 80th percentile, have all the skills necessary to take the most advanced math and science courses in high school and college.
- Gifted girls may perform better in math or science classes that are taught by women and include many or all female students.
- Gifted girls may find it easier to learn math and science when they are able to apply the ideas to people-oriented problems.
- Girls should ask teachers for examples that are relevant to their lives rather than examples related to sports or mechanics, which may not be relevant to their experiences.

Counselors should be aware that it is not only in math and science that gifted girls often take fewer and less rigorous courses. Results of Kerr and Colangelo's ACT studies (1988) show that even in the social studies girls tend to achieve lower scores on tests of curricular knowledge than do boys. This means that gifted girls may tend to take the less difficult social studies course, such as "The Sixties" or "Marriage and Family," rather than "Western Civilization."

In order to preserve gifted girls' future choices, counselors need to ensure that the girls take the fullest and most challenging course load available in high school. Wherever advanced coursework is not available in the high school, the counselor should help the gifted girl and her parents to locate community college or university coursework that she can take in order to supplement her in-class learning.

Advisement for gifted girls should also include encouragement to take summer courses and to participate in special camps and institutes for gifted students. Gifted girls may be reluctant to take part in these activities for gifted students because they perceive that summer opportunities for gifted students lack social activities. In addition, they may be anxious about making new friends and leaving their familiar environment and friends. Counselors need to give these girls courage, and to show them how these activities can help them form their goals and achieve entrance into colleges and universities that will develop their talents.

Counselors should collect information on special institutes, camps, and school-year activities for the gifted and talented and discuss this information with gifted girls, who may not take as much initiative as would gifted boys in seeking these opportunities.

## Increasing Social Self-Esteem

According to Hollinger and Fleming (1988), social self-esteem is related both to academic achievement and life satisfaction. Social self-esteem is made up of two self-perceptions: instrumentality and expressiveness. Women with high instrumentality are decisive, active, and prone to risk taking, whereas those with high expressiveness are caring, communicative, and affiliative. A combination of both these characteristics seems to be necessary for girls to feel good about themselves.

How can counselors help to increase girls' expressiveness and instrumentality? Expressiveness tends to be a characteristic more commonly found among women than men. Gifted girls need to be accepting of the expressive aspects of their personality. Counselors need to show gifted girls that it is possible to be assertive and achieving and still be expressive and emotional. Instrumentality can be increased through leadership opportunities, development of decision-making skills, and the participation in challenging activities. Too often in extracurricular activities and sports, boys take the leadership positions. Girls need a chance to lead classroom groups, to captain sports teams, and to be decision makers in clubs and groups. Counselors may want to consider leading assertiveness groups and decision-making groups for gifted girls who seem particularly shy or reluctant to take leadership positions.

Biographical information about eminent women shows clearly that as girls these women were not necessarily quiet and well-behaved; often, they were quite the opposite. Counselors may need to be the advocate and friend for nonconforming or rebellious gifted girls. It may be that these young women's assertiveness and independence will protect them from discrimination and enhance the possibility of achieving of their goals.

## Identity Development

Another finding derived from the lives of eminent women is that the development of identity is critical to later achievement. Bloom's (1985) study of eminent concert pianists, Olympic athletes, and sculptors showed that these people had an opportunity as early as in adolescence to identify themselves and to be identified as the "class artist" or the "school athlete." To develop a strong identity in a talent area, a gifted girl first needs to know specific objective information about how she compares to others in that area, and second, she needs to be reinforced in that identity.

Counselors can help by using objective test information to underscore a girl's talent. For instance, a counselor might say "You have scored in the 95th percentile in verbal reasoning. This means that 95% of the rest of the young people in the nation have less ability than you do to get good grades in English and to succeed in language-related careers." To reinforce a gifted girl, a counselor might say "So you've achieved an A in math again. You're really the math whiz around here!" It is also helpful to encourage other students to recognize the specific talents of the gifted girl.

It is important to seek ways in which bright girls can receive recognition for their special abilities. Kaufmann (1981) found that most of the Presidential Scholars had received very little in the way of recognition as high school students; some believed that the failure of their high school peers, teachers, and counselors to notice or acknowledge their academic abilities had led them to discounting their own skills. Those bright girls who receive formal awards and prizes as well as informal friendly recognition of their talents are more likely to continue their high achievement.

## Helping Gifted Girls With Relationships

Gifted adolescent girls and gifted women may experience problems in their relationships. Like all adolescents, gifted girls experience frustration, anxiety, and depression when they fail to have the kinds of relationships they want. All adolescents are searching for someone to love and to be loved by. However, gifted girls may suffer from their own unique dilemmas related to their giftedness. It is a fact that in our society men are attracted to women who are their intellectual equals or their inferiors whereas women are attracted to men who are their intellectual equals or superiors. In plain language, what this means for gifted heterosexual girls is a much smaller group of potential partners from which to choose. It is wrong to deny that gifted girls will have more difficulty in establishing relationships with boys (Kerr, 1985) than will nongifted girls.

One study showed that although the majority of gifted girls expected to have careers, only a small percentage of gifted boys expected their wives to work (Fox, 1976). Gifted boys' images of the ideal girl may be at odds with the reality of the gifted girls with whom they share their classes.

Unrealistic expectations on the part of both gifted young women and young men may block them from satisfying friendships. Bright girls tend to be achievement-oriented and some are perfectionistic. They may treat romantic relationships as if they were achievements. They may have overly high expectations of relationships. Perfectionistic young women may seek "the perfect guy." When relationships don't work out, gifted girls may feel as if they have failed. Having little experience with failure in any other realm of their lives, they can be disconcerted and frightened by rejection.

Gifted young women are often unaware of the fact that a single lifestyle has been a satisfying and fulfilling one for many gifted women. In fact, single, childless women were among the most satisfied in Sears and Barbee's (1977) follow-up of elderly gifted women.

Young lesbian gifted women bear the double burden of their society's negative attitude toward giftedness as well as society's negative attitude toward their sexual orientation. They may feel particularly isolated and unsure about relationships. They are often unaware of the lives of adult lesbians and the possibilities of happy, stable relationships and supportive women's communities.

Counselors can provide realistic assessments of relationships and a sympathetic ear. Counselors may also want to consider relationship education specifically for gifted girls. Again, the lives of eminent women can often provide models for healthy relationships and partnerships. Most eminent women who have achieved success in their work and happiness in their intimate relationships are those who have based their relationships on deeply held values. These are women who seem to have found partners through their work. Although eminent women do not necessarily have partners in the same career areas, they tend to have partners who value their work and who share a style that allows a life of working together (Kerr, 1985).

Perhaps the most difficult situation the counselor may encounter in working with the gifted girl is one in which the girl is in danger of giving up academic and career opportunities in order to hold on to a boyfriend. Bright girls have attended inferior colleges, rejected scholarships, withdrawn from challenging classes, and even dropped out of high school in order to preserve relationships. Careful and caring guidance is needed to prevent bright girls from making decisions that will sabotage their own dreams and goals.

## Helping Gifted Girls to Fall in Love With an Idea

Perhaps the most important common theme in the lives of eminent women is that of "falling in love with an idea." Torrance (1979) defined falling in love with an idea as committing oneself to a deeply held value, a theory, or an attitude. Falling in love with an idea is the same as the process of discovering one's calling or one's vocation. People who love an idea have a deep sense of purpose. Many of the distresses gifted girls and young women face can be lightened if they have developed a deep sense of purpose. Similar to identity development, falling in love with an idea requires that the gifted girl understand her specific talent. Sometimes it is necessary for the counselor to point out how passionately a gifted girl feels about a particular activity even before the girl herself realizes her involvement with it.

Statements such as, "Kathy, your poetry shows an enormous amount of hard work. You really love creative writing, don't you?" Or, "Beth, I can see that most of your activities center around leadership. You like your courses in government and psychology and you like all your student government activities. Leadership is really an important theme in your life. I hope that you are considering a career that allows you to lead others because you have the talent and the passion for it." In this way, gifted girls are given permission to fall in love with an idea and get the help they sometimes need to nurture that process.

Value-based career counseling, a technique developed at The University of Iowa's Counseling Laboratory for Talent Development (Kerr & Erb, in press), is particularly helpful in discovering ideas worth falling in love with. Value-based career counseling can help girls to raise their aspirations; to focus on future goals; to analyze the role of relationships in their career development; to understand how their interests, needs, and values make them unique; and finally, to understand the importance of choosing a career based on deeply held values. The counselor who helps the gifted girl to fall in love with an idea has given the greatest gift that a counselor can give a bright and promising young woman.

## Summary

Although gifted adolescent girls now have higher aspirations than did gifted girls of the past, they continue to be unsure of their goals, to make unwise course-taking decisions, and sometimes to subordinate their career goals to relationships. Counselors can help girls to achieve their full potential by assisting in identification of the gifted; helping teachers achieve equity in the classroom; providing career education and career workshops; offering careful advising; increasing social self-esteem; developing identity; and helping gifted girls to fall in love with an idea.

## References

Benbow, C. P., & Stanley, J. C. (1984). Gender and the science major: A study of mathematically precocious youth. In M. W. Steinkamp & M. L. Maehr (Eds.), *Women in science* (pp. 165–196). Greenwich, CT: JAI Press.

Bloom, B. S. (1985). *Developing talent in young people.* New York: Ballantine Books.

Callahan, C. M. (1979). The gifted and talented woman. In A. H. Passow (Ed.), *The gifted and talented: Their education and development.* The seventy-eighth yearbook of the National Society of the Study of Education, Part 1 (pp. 401–423). Chicago, IL: University of Chicago Press.

Chan, L. K. S. (1988). The perceived competence of intellectually talented students. *Gifted Child Quarterly, 32*(3), 310–315.

Colangelo, N., & Kerr, B. A. (1990). Extreme academic talent: Profiles of perfect scorers. *Journal of Educational Psychology, 82*(3). 404–409.

Doolittle, A. E., & Cleary, T. A. (1987). Gender-biased item performance in math achievement items. *Journal of Educational Measurement, 24*(2), 157–166.

Fleming, E., & Hollinger, C. (1979). *Project choice: Creating her options in career education.* Cleveland, OH: ERIC Reproduction Service No. EO185321.

Fox, L. H. (1976). *Changing behaviors and attitudes of gifted girls.* Paper presented at the American Psychological Association, Washington, DC.

Gardner, H. (1983). *Frames of mind: The theory of multiple intelligences.* New York: Basic Books.

Gilligan, C. (1982). *In a different voice: Psychological theory and women's development.* Cambridge, MA: Harvard University Press.

Groth, N. J. (1969). *Vocational development for gifted girls.* ERIC Document Reproduction Service No. ED931747.

Hollinger, C. L. (1983). Counseling the gifted and talented female adolescent: The relationship between social self-esteem and traits of instrumentality and expressiveness. *Gifted Child Quarterly, 27*(4), 157–161.

Hollinger, C. L., & Fleming, E. S. (1984). Internal barriers to the realization of potential: Correlates and interrelationships among gifted and talented female adolescents. *Journal of Youth and Adolescence, 14*(5), 389–399.

Hollinger, C. L., & Fleming, E. S. (1988). Gifted and talented young women: Antecedents and correlates of life satisfaction. *Gifted Child Quarterly, 32*(2), 254–259.

Jacobs, J. E., & Eccles, J. S. (1985, March). Gender differences in math ability: The impact of media reports on parents. *Educational Researcher,* pp. 20–24.

Kaufmann, F. (1981). The 1964–1968 Presidential Scholars: A follow-up study. *Exceptional Children, 48,* 2.

Kelly, K., & Colangelo, N. (1984). Academic and social self-concepts of gifted, general, and special students. *Exceptional Children, 50,* 551–553.

Kerr, B. A. (1983). Raising aspirations of gifted girls. *Vocational Guidance Quarterly, 32,* 37–44.

Kerr, B. A. (1985). *Smart girls, gifted women.* Columbus, OH: Ohio Psychology.

Kerr, B. A., & Colangelo, N. (1988). The college plans of academically talented students. *Journal of Counseling and Development, 67*(1), 42–49.

Kerr, B. A., Colangelo, N., & Gaeth, J. (1988). Gifted adolescents' attitudes toward their giftedness. *Gifted Child Quarterly, 32*(2), 245–248.

Kerr, B. A., & Erb, C. (in press). Career counseling for gifted students. Effects of value-based intervention. *Journal of Counseling Psychology.*

Laing, J., Engen, H., & Maxey, J. (1987). The relationship of high school coursework to corresponding ACT assessment scores. *ACT Research Report, 87*–3. Iowa City, IA: American College Testing Program.

Ludwig, G., & Cullinan, D. (1984). Behavior problems of gifted and nongifted elementary school girls and boys. *Gifted Child Quarterly, 28*(1), 37–40.

Sadker, D., & Sadker, M. (1984, March). *Year II, Final Report, promoting effectiveness in classroom instruction.* Washington, DC: NIE Contract 400-80-0033.

Sadker, D., & Sadker, M. (1985, April). *Interventions that promote equity and effectiveness in student-teacher interaction.* Paper presented at the annual meeting of the American Education Research Association, Chicago, IL.

Sears, P. S., & Barbee, A. H. (1977). Career and life satisfactions among Terman's gifted women. In J. C. Stanley, W. C. George, & C. H. Solano (Eds.), *The gifted and creative: A fifty year perspective* (pp. 28–65). Baltimore, MD: Johns Hopkins Press.

Silverman, L. K. (1986). What happens in the gifted girl? In C. J. Maker (Ed.), *Critical issues in gifted education: Defensible programs for the gifted* (pp. 43–89). Rockville, MD: Aspen.

Solano, C. H. (1977). Teacher and pupil stereotypes of gifted boys and girls. *Talents and Gifts, 19*, 4.

Sternberg, R. J., & Davidson, J. E. (1986). *Conceptions of giftedness.* New York: Cambridge University Press.

Terman, L. M., & Oden, M. H. (1935). The promise of youth. *Genetic studies of genius,* Vol. 3. Stanford, CA: Stanford University Press.

Torrance, E. P. (1979). *The search for satori and creativity.* Greatneck, NY: Creative Synergetic Associates.

# Psychological Adjustment of Gifted Students

Psychologists have long tried to understand the relationship of intelligence to psychological adjustment. For many centuries madness and genius were considered to be inextricably linked. Our culture holds many stereotypes of gifted individuals, most of them negative. Images of gifted people in the media have ranged from the bumbling absent-minded professor to the hard-drinking writer or half-crazed artist.

Terman hoped to put these negative images of gifted individuals to rest with his research. However, in many ways, Terman's studies of gifted individuals raised as many questions as they answered. Although Terman found that the majority of the students identified by his procedures grew up to be well-adjusted adults, among the group there were indeed people who had suffered psychological disorders (Terman & Oden, 1947). There were instances of depression, anxiety, and even suicides among the group. Apparently, too, at the highest IQ levels, there were more psychological disorders than would be expected in a normal group.

Leta Hollingworth (1942) also provided support for the idea that at the highest levels of ability gifted students may simply be too different from average students to ever lead normal lives. Her students with IQs above 180, although for the most part functioning well, had suffered a great deal from being treated as deviants in the classroom and in society.

In more recent years, research on the psychological adjustment of gifted individuals has become more sophisticated and has begun to explore more complex questions than simply ''Are gifted students well adjusted?'' It is common now for studies to examine a wide variety of characteristics associated with psychological adjustment such as self-concept, self-actualizing tendencies, depression, and social self-esteem. In addition, contemporary studies of gifted students examine the adjustment of boys and girls, of students of varying ages, of students of differing abilities, and of students in particular talent areas.

In this chapter, we will first explore differing subpopulations of gifted students, and second, we will examine some common adjustment disorders that may affect gifted students. Interventions will be suggested for some of these adjustment disorders.

## Gender and Adjustment

The majority of studies of gifted girls and boys show that gifted girls are better adjusted than gifted boys or average girls and boys. On personality measures, gifted girls show fewer traits associated with poor adjustment such as depression and anxiety. Also, gifted girls are referred for fewer behavior disorders than gifted boys or average girls and boys (Kerr, 1985). Only in the matter of self-concept some findings indicate that gifted girls may have a lower opinion of themselves than gifted boys. Most studies show that both gifted boys and girls have positive self-concepts (Kelly & Colangelo, 1990). However, when self-concept is considered in terms of academic and social self-concept, some complexities emerge. For instance, gifted girls may have a lower social self-concept as a result of being labeled gifted; many gifted girls feel that giftedness is actually a social handicap (Kerr, Colangelo, & Gaeth, 1987). Most studies find that gifted boys and girls have about the same academic self-concept, but some studies show that gifted girls have less confidence in their academic abilities than their actual achievement would warrant.

Hollinger and Fleming (1985) suggested that because social self-esteem in gifted girls seems to be the result of a combination of masculine and feminine characteristics, androgyny may be the best predictor of social adjustment for the gifted girl. Other studies have found that gifted girls who are less conforming to social norms than girls in general tend to be psychologically healthier. One study (Karnes & Wherry, 1983) found that gifted girls were more casual and careless than other girls, and other studies have found gifted girls to be more independent, curious, and assertive.

In short, gifted girls and boys are very similar in their personality characteristics because they tend to be superior to average students in their psychological adjustment. Differences occur in the areas of social self-concept or social self-esteem, and differences favoring boys tend to appear only during the adolescent years when girls may be particularly sensitive to the social impact of giftedness. Although many studies examine specific personality characteristics such as dominance, need for achievement, or depression, there are too many conflicting data to be able to make any statement about specific characteristics of gifted girls and boys. After reviewing the studies comparing boys' and girls' personality characteristics and psychological adjustment, it can be said that Terman's finding probably still holds true: Gifted girls and boys are more like each other psychologically than they are different, and both are well adjusted.

## Age and Adjustment

Although only a few longitudinal studies exist that trace the adjustment of gifted individuals over the course of long periods of time, most of these studies (Terman & Oden, 1947; Kaufmann, 1981) agree that gifted individuals in general are well adjusted throughout the life span. However, there may be critical periods for gifted students just as there are for average students when mistimed interventions or lack of intervention can lead to adjustment problems. Preschool and kindergarten can be a difficult time for many gifted children. As Stephanie Tolan pointed out in her case study in *Guiding the Gifted Child* (Webb, Meckstroth, & Tolan, 1982), gifted children may be sorely surprised upon finding that their preschool or kindergarten playmates cannot play the same games or read the same books they themselves can.

Many gifted children look forward to the beginning of preschool or kindergarten with great enthusiasm and anticipation. They are often disappointed, frustrated, and bored with the reality of school. As a result, gifted children may develop school-related problems such as fear or anxiety about going to school; quarrelling with playmates; or withdrawal into fantasy or daydreaming during the school day.

Gifted 4- to 7-year-olds may have a difficult time understanding why other children cannot keep up with them and why teachers fail to stimulate them to the degree that they need. This is a period of life that requires patient understanding and guidance from parents, teachers, and counselors.

Another critical period for many gifted students is the entry into junior high school (Buescher, 1987). Gifted students may begin to be especially sensitive about being labeled gifted in junior high, particularly girls. Both boys and girls may see their giftedness as a social disadvantage. In addition, new social and romantic interests may overwhelm the previously intellectually oriented child, bringing about what seems to be a marked change in personality.

Teachers frustrated by the sudden onset of silly or blindly conforming behavior may believe that there are adjustment problems above and beyond those caused by the onset of adolescence. However, in most cases, it is simply the contrast between the intense achievement orientation that was once directed toward academic work and that is now directed toward social accomplishments and popularity, which leads the gifted students, teachers, and parents to be alarmed by this change in behavior (Groth, 1969).

Another critical period is also a transitional period: the end of senior year and the beginning of college. Many gifted students at this point become afflicted with indecision and fears about the future. In chapter 5 on career counseling for the gifted and talented, it was noted that multipotentiality can be a source of great difficulty for gifted students; having too many options can be a curse rather than a blessing. This confusion, toward the end of the senior year, can sometimes lead to depression, anxiety, and the lowering of academic performance after years of success (Frederickson & Rothney, 1972).

The beginning of the freshman year of college brings with it, often for the first time, competition with students of equal and superior intellectual ability. This often leads to dismay and anger in the gifted student who is used to straight A's and little competition. Some students who have never experienced failure may be intensely negatively affected by every grade less than an A. Occasionally, the fear of failure can lead students to deliberately underachieve, to withdraw from college completely, or to choose another college with much lower standards.

## Talent Area and Adjustment

There is good reason to believe that certain psychological characteristics may be linked to particular talent areas. John Holland's work established that vocational interest areas were strongly related to personality characteristics (Gottfredson & Holland, 1989). There has been a great deal of controversy about the ways in which ability and personality may be related. Interest in characteristics of individuals with specific talents has grown since Gardner's (1983) theory of multiple intelligences, and Bloom's (1985) study of gifted adults in specific talent areas. In addition, evidence from programs such as the Study of Mathematically Precocious Youth and the Study for Verbally Precocious Youth at Johns Hopkins as well as the many Governor's Institutes that select students in specific talent areas has shown that some fairly predictable psychological characteristics and adjustment problems are related to specific talent areas.

## Verbally Gifted Students

Verbally gifted students' advanced vocabulary and unusual fluency can actually make it difficult for them to relate to others (Webb et al., 1982). Whenever verbally gifted students find themselves in conversations with individuals of lower verbal ability, they may be constantly trimming their conversation to fit the group. Particularly tactful verbally gifted students may conscientiously avoid using long words and discussing topics about which their agemates are ignorant. However, years of attempting to relate to people of lesser verbal ability may transform the talkative and friendly gifted student into a sarcastic cynic.

Verbally gifted students are particularly challenging as clients. As counselors, we often assume that the ability to articulate one's problems is equal to the ability to solve one's problems. This is simply not true with these students. They may be able to label and describe their difficulties eloquently, and yet not have the slightest notion of how to go about resolving them. Verbally gifted students literally talk around their problems.

Studies at Johns Hopkins University have shown that verbally gifted students may experience more psychological difficulties than mathematically gifted students (Brody & Benbow, 1986). When verbally gifted students have problems that merit referral to counseling, they are more likely than students in other talent areas to be witty, rebellious, and argumentative. The counselor may find it necessary to use counseling techniques that are less verbal; it may be useless to attempt to beat the client at his or her own game. Gestalt techniques (Perls, Hefferline, & Goodman, 1951) and other techniques that emphasize experience and awareness rather than conversation may be more appropriate.

Finally, it may be that verbally gifted students suffer the most from lack of acceleration and opportunities for intellectual stimulation. Their lively minds and their desire to describe and discuss every aspect of their existence may be thwarted by the lack of opportunity to read challenging books, to engage in conversation with intellectual peers and superiors, and to argue and debate at a high level.

## Mathematically Gifted Students

Studies of mathematically gifted students have dispelled the myth that they are awkward and socially inept (Haier & Denham, 1976). There is little evidence that mathematically gifted students are withdrawn or alienated. Mathematicians and scientists do tend to be more introverted by nature, according to vocational interest studies (Gottfredson & Holland, 1989). However, mathematically gifted students' introversion is likely to be well within the normal range.

Nevertheless, there are those mathematically gifted students whose interests are so esoteric that they may indeed be rejected by other children who have little understanding of the mathematical concepts that the gifted student finds so fascinating. In addition, many mathematically gifted students may actually choose the label of ''brain'' or ''nerd'' because paradoxically, the media have made it somewhat fashionable in the 1990s to be brilliant in an area such as math, chess, or computers. Movies such as ''Stand and Deliver,'' ''The Wizard,'' and ''Back to the Future'' provide models of young people who are fascinated by math and science activities. Therefore, counselors and teachers should not automatically assume that a student who is considered ''weird'' by his or her peers is necessarily unpopular or unliked.

More critical to the psychological adjustment of mathematically gifted students than social popularity may be the issue of acceleration and intellectual challenge. Because mathematical giftedness often appears at a very early age (Gardner, 1983), these students need guidance and education even in the elementary grades. Mathematical knowledge is logical and linear in its progression, and is well suited to acceleration. Mathematically gifted students often have an intense desire for further information about their interests as well as an intuitive sense that there is much more to know. The refusal of schools or parents to allow the mathematically gifted child to learn at his or her own pace may lead not only to frustration and anxiety but also to the eventual rejection of math interests. Mathematically talented students must be nurtured and encouraged in their interests. Attempts to make them well rounded by discouraging math interests and encouraging participation in intellectual and social activities that are less attractive to these students are probably doomed to failure.

Counseling with mathematically gifted students may require that the counselor become knowledgeable about some of the mathematical ideas that are fascinating to the students. This does not mean that the counselor needs to be mathematically gifted; merely that he or she be willing to show curiosity rather than ignorance in the face of the client's enthusiasm. Most counseling strategies that rely upon sound reasoning such as rational-emotive therapy (Ellis & Harper, 1975) may be particularly well suited to mathematically gifted students who are experiencing psychological difficulties.

## Spatially-Visually Gifted Students

The spatially-visually gifted student literally sees what others don't see, and this experience can be isolating. The spatially-visually gifted student may often think in images rather than in words (Gardner, 1983). These students' visual talents may be manifested most obviously in their dress and grooming. At the Nebraska Scholars' Institute, one instructor was heard to say of the Integrated Arts group of students, "You can see them coming a block away by the way they are dressed." Perhaps it's their tendency to think in images and to dress in unusual ways that leads to the stereotype of spatially-visually gifted students as nonconformists. However, the vast majority of spatially-visually gifted students are not nonconforming socially; they are, however, nonconforming in the way they perceive and think.

Critics and those who appreciate the arts are often frustrated by artists' inability to articulate the meaning or purpose of their works. This is because artists simply feel little need for verbal explanations. Images for the spatially-visually gifted students stand by themselves and have meaning in themselves. As a result, when spatially-visually gifted students do have psychological problems, they are most commonly related to problems in communicating their feelings or thoughts to other people in ways that others can understand.

Counselors need to think of creative ways of helping spatially-visually gifted students to express themselves. Psychodrama (Moreno, 1946–1969) and art therapy techniques may be particularly useful in counseling and therapy with spatially-visually gifted students.

In chapter 3 on underachievement, it was noted that one of the most common reasons for the diagnosis of underachievement is actually the result of a misunderstanding of the IQ or achievement test scores of spatially-visually gifted individuals. Spatially-visually gifted students often score quite remarkably on the WISC-R performance scale and other nonverbal measures of intellectual ability, but achieve only average or above-average scores on measures of verbal ability. These students are not true underachievers. It is simply the case that the curriculum of most schools offers little that taps the abilities of the spatially-visually gifted student. Only in such areas as art, photography, geography, and geometry are spatially-visually gifted students likely to shine. Therefore counselors must be on the lookout for this misdiagnosis and must also be prepared to deal with the effects of a mistaken assessment. Students who are spatially-visually gifted but only average in verbal abilities may be misplaced in gifted education programs or incorrectly accelerated in verbal talent areas.

## Musically Gifted Students

The problems and psychological characteristics unique to musically gifted students are probably directly linked to the nature of the development of talented musicians. Musical talent, in order to flourish as musical accomplishment, requires rehearsal and training usually from a very early age (Bloom, 1985). Music is an area in which creativity and panache cannot substitute for hard work and long practice. Musically gifted students, like mathematically gifted students, may show their talent at an extremely early age (Gardner, 1983). These students can be identified and given training while still very young. Whereas acceleration for verbally, mathematically, and spatially-visually gifted children is extremely rare, acceleration for musically gifted students, usually through private schooling, is common. Musically gifted students usually progress through the learning of music at the rate that is appropriate to the level of their talent. Occasionally, however, musically gifted students may feel pressured to work faster and with more complex pieces than they feel ready for. Performance anxiety and a dread of practice can result.

Students who seem obsessed and completely involved with music may have a love-hate relationship with their instrument or talent. They may feel consumed by the discipline that is necessary. They may feel as if their lives are being shaped by the inanimate object with which they must spend so much time if they are instrumental musicians. In addition, many musically gifted students must suffer through long periods in which their talent may not be recognized or rewarded. Although there is frequently a role as an accompanist for the child who plays the piano and an occasional performance for children playing other instruments, much of the musical giftedness of these children seems irrelevant in the regular school curriculum. Because musical talent does not always go along with academic talent, these students may feel as if their own gift has somehow been devalued.

When musically gifted students come for counseling or therapy, they may show the same kinds of inarticulateness that counselors sometimes experience in spatially-visually gifted students. Musically gifted students may think in musical terms sometimes. It may be easier for them to describe an emotion musically than verbally. One harpsicord player who came to the Guidance Laboratory for Gifted and Talented needing help with depression asked her counselor to meet with her in her practice room at the music building so that she could express to her in music the emotions she could not discuss. The counselor then was able to help her find words for her feelings. Music therapy techniques may be particularly helpful.

## Interpersonally Gifted Students

Interpersonally gifted students are likely to be well adjusted, almost by definition (Gardner, 1983). However, occasionally interpersonally gifted students can have problems related to their gifts of empathy, communication skills, and ability to influence others. As discussed in chapter 3 on underachievement, interpersonally gifted students sometimes receive high grades and excellent recommendations from teachers based mainly upon their outstanding communication skills. This may lead to problems when the student is confronted with objective tests of his or her verbal reasoning ability, mathematical skills, or other skills that are not as well developed as "people" skills.

Interpersonally gifted students may also have difficulty with career development. Because they are often very socially oriented, interpersonally gifted students may be drawn to a wide variety of socially oriented careers or professions. However, they may lack good career exploration skills or decision-making skills.

In counseling, the interpersonally gifted student may present a number of unique problems. Often, interpersonally gifted students have many of the same skills that counselors have; this can be a jarring experience. At the Guidance Laboratory for Gifted and Talented, we have often observed that interpersonally gifted students seem to "mirror" the counselor's behavior. These students tended to listen, to engage in empathic responding, and to repeat and rephrase what the counselor was saying. Sometimes these clients are extremely dominant or manipulative during the session. In counseling, a client who is able to draw out the counselor or to manipulate the counselor may not get his or her needs met. Therefore, the counselor needs to make a special effort to make the interpersonally gifted student the center of the counseling procedure and to insist that he or she stay on task during the process of decision making. Gestalt techniques, which frustrate clients' manipulations, are helpful.

## Psychological Adjustment and Educational Placement

One of the most common and widespread misconceptions about gifted education is that grouping and acceleration lead to problems in psychological adjustment. A common criticism of special grouping for the gifted is that grouping students according to ability leads to elitism. In addition, the claim is often made that grouping gifted students leads to overly high expectations, pressuring, and competitiveness. This notion persists despite the fact that there is little research evidence to support this idea. In fact, the vast majority of studies contradict the notion that grouping is related to psychological adjustment disorders (Lehman & Erdwins, 1981).

On the contrary, grouping seems to benefit bright students by increasing their intellectual stimulation and providing opportunities for friendships with intellectual peers. Directors of Talent Search programs and Governor's Institute programs frequently have observed that students who enter summer programs with a record of behavior or personality disorders often seem to improve spontaneously in their behavior in an environment that encourages academic challenge and relationships with other bright students.

The idea that grouping students leads to elitism among gifted students has also received no support from research. Studies of the Iowa Governor's Institute showed that students who participated in this institute tended to improve in the areas of self-esteem and social support, feeling more self-confident and more comfortable in relationships with other students than before participating in the institute (Kerr, Hallowell, & Erb, 1989).

Gifted students need to learn to be comfortable and on friendly terms with people of much lesser ability. In order for gifted students to learn to be tolerant and even compassionate toward students of lesser ability, it is necessary for them to feel comfortable with their own abilities and to have empathy for the feelings of inferiority or failure that so many average and less-than-average students experience.

Paradoxically, it may be that retaining a gifted student in a regular classroom throughout the school years can lead to elitism and contemptuousness. A student who has always received the highest grades in the class and has found all tasks to be easy, and who has been prevented from understanding his or her giftedness, may assume that success is simply the result of hard work. For this student, it follows that the other students in the class are simply not working hard enough. It is much more likely that a student who perceives his or her peers as lazy or unmotivated will grow contemptuous rather than a student who perceives his or her peers to be of lesser ability.

On the other hand, a gifted student who has been placed in an appropriately challenging gifted program may learn for the first time what it means *not* to be as competent as other students. That student learns what it feels like to not be the best. Placement in a gifted program with one's intellectual peers can be a humbling experience, although in the long run a growth-producing one.

Acceleration has also received much condemnation as a source of pressure and psychological disorders. Again, however, the research on acceleration has shown the effect of this educational strategy to be precisely the opposite (Janos & Robinson, 1986; Kulik & Kulik, 1983). Most studies of accelerated students show them to be better adjusted than their nonaccelerated peers. Even among students who have been accelerated as much as by 5 or 6 years, such as the students in Talent Search programs and radical accelerants who are admitted early to colleges and universities, these findings hold true. Acceleration may be harmful only to students who are misplaced because of inappropriate evaluation of their abilities or to students who have other behavior and personality disorders unrelated to their giftedness.

Because the findings that support grouping and acceleration of gifted students go against the intuitions and inclinations of so many policymakers, information about these research findings usually fall on deaf ears. Gifted educators and counselors who have read the research and who have observed gifted students in accelerated programs or programs for gifted students are often frustrated by their inability to communicate this information. Nevertheless, counselors have as great a responsibility to dispel misconceptions about gifted students and gifted programming as they have to dispel the many myths about minority and handicapped children that have prevented them from receiving appropriate educational opportunities.

## Common Adjustment Disorders of Gifted Students

In this section, the common adjustment disorders gifted students experience will be discussed. Stress-related problems, depression, perfectionism, and problems in relationships are probably the most frequently cited presenting problems of bright students.

## Stress and the Gifted Student

Jessie is a 6-year-old girl who likes to read the newspaper. Soon after she reads several accounts of people who have been poisoned by medicines that have been tampered with, she begins to have nightmares about poisoning. Soon she insists that her mother check all of her food to be sure that it doesn't have poison in it.

Lynn has just been admitted to a special school for the gifted. She is happy and proud to be in the gifted school because she knows that her parents are happy about it. Soon after her admittance, however, she develops a number of nervous habits such as nail biting. Worst of all, she begins to lose her hair; the only diagnosis the family doctor gives is that she is nervous and anxious.

Jordan is a member of the high school swim team and is its high-point diver. He is also a straight-A student and the editor of the high school newspaper. One day Jordan doesn't show up for swim practice. He has no explanation or excuse when the coach stops him in the hall, but he refuses to swim again.

All three of these students are gifted children under stress. There are as many reasons for gifted students to experience stress as there are sources of stress. However, some aspects of giftedness seem to be particularly conducive to stress, particularly loneliness (Kaiser & Berndt, 1985) and academic stress (Yadusky-Holahan & Holahan, 1983). It is interesting how often people immediately assume that the gifted student under stress is being "pushed" by his or her parents. Many writers have castigated parents and teachers for having overly high expectations of gifted students and have attempted to show a relationship between these expectations and the students' experience of stress. There is indeed some truth to the notion that stress can be related to overly high expectations; however, this alone is not a satisfactory explanation. Some students with ambitious, hard-driving parents nevertheless are relaxed and easy-going. On the other hand, every teacher has seen a gifted student who seems tremendously anxious and success-oriented but who has casual, easy-going parents with only the most moderate expectations of their child. It is not likely that parental pressure alone is the cause of stress in the gifted child.

For some gifted children, however, meeting others' expectations has become a way of life (Kerr, 1982). The student who is expected, not only by parents but also by teachers, school administrators, and community to be achievement-oriented may indeed feel pressure. The small town "scholar-athlete"; the high school's star speech and debate student who has won a national contest; or the school's only national merit scholar all may feel pressure as a result of their unique status. Jim Delisle, in his book, *Gifted Children Speak Out* (1984), gave many examples of students' beliefs that others hold expectations of them that are too high. Many gifted students describe a cycle in which achievement is followed by expectation of higher achievement, which is then followed by higher achievement in a never-ending spiral, so that the student believes that no matter how much he or she may try, no attainment will ever be enough.

How can the gifted student break out of this vicious cycle? How can counselors help the student out of the cycle? One of the only ways of helping gifted students to deal with the overly high expectations of others is to help them to move from extrinsic motivation to intrinsic motivation. Extrinsic motivation, the dependence on others' approval, recognition, and rewards, can be a trap. When explicit approval or reward is not present, the student may become extremely anxious, looking around for a way of evaluating his or her performance. Intrinsic motivation, on the other hand, is characterized by self-evaluation and an independence from the opinions of others. Students who have internalized their own set of standards can judge their own performance. Because they do not need to rely on the opinions of others for self-evaluation, they can be more autonomous and more confident about their performance. Counselors can help bright students to develop intrinsic motivation by challenging them to evaluate their own performance. For example, when reviewing a student's transcript, the counselor can point to each course and grade and say, ''You received an A in French. Is this the grade that you expected? Is this the grade that you believe you deserved?'' Or ''Here is a B in pre-calculus. How would you have evaluated your performance? To what degree were you challenging yourself?'' It is important for the counselor to help the student to decide upon the level of effort that he or she will consider satisfactory, rather than the actual outcome that the student will consider satisfactory.

What happens, however, when students set their own internal standards too high? This, too, is a serious source of stress. Many gifted students seem to ''raise the stakes'' on their own, even when parents and teachers assure them that their performance is excellent. These students never seem to be satisfied with any amount of recognition or reward. Each accomplishment merely sets the stage for the next effort. Some internal force presses these students toward achievement. It is not achievement orientation per se that is stressful. In fact, most eminent individuals drive themselves very hard and are extraordinarily persistent in their work. Many accomplished adults are extremely self-critical. Stress results when there is no area of the student's life that is not counted as a potential achievement and when the student is completely indiscriminating about accomplishments. Being focused on excellence in a major area of interest is seldom as stressful as a student's desire to be perfect in all activities.

Another common source of stress in the lives of gifted adolescents is overcommitment to school activities. Many gifted boys and girls seem to be engaged in a fierce competition to see who can receive the most inches of fine print under their names in the yearbook. Multipotential students, with multiple interests and skills, often seem to find themselves involved in nearly every extracurricular activity available (Kerr, 1982). Too often, students have been encouraged by faculty advisors to participate in activities such as yearbook, plays, newspaper, athletics, pep squad, and departmental clubs without an awareness of the degree of their involvement in other activities. The bright young man who cannot say no to any after-school activity may suddenly find himself in a position of having multiple conflicting commitments. Teenagers who find themselves constantly having to be two or three places at once and need to seek excuses from classes in order to fulfill out-of-class obligations may begin to experience all their activities as stressful. Some gifted students begin to resemble middle-aged, overly harassed executives, rushing from one appointment to the next and suffering from stress-related symptoms. Headaches, stomach disturbances and ulcers, skin rashes, and respiratory disorders all have stress as a common denominator. The remedy for these stress symptoms is exactly the same as that recommended for the hard-driving executive: a change in life-style.

Bright students who have become overextended need help in learning how to manage their time more effectively and to set priorities on their activities. Counselors can help best by engaging them in time management exercises. Also, students can be helped to rank their activities in a variety of ways. First, they can rank their activities in order of preference; second, in terms of each activity's value in applying to college; and third, in order of each activity's importance to the school. The counselor can help the student discuss these rankings and develop a final list.

In general, these students need to learn how to slow down. They need help finding time for rest, for proper eating, and for recreation. Many of these bright, hard-working students almost seem to have forgotten how to play. Counselors need to encourage them to let go of some of their structured activities and replace them with more unstructured, spontaneous activities.

Finally, an important source of stress in the lives of many gifted students is the necessity of making decisions that are simply beyond their capacity to make (Kerr, 1982). The third grader who is asked to make his own decision about whether to enter a gifted program; the seventh-grade girl who has to make a decision whether to stay home for the summer or to attend an institute for the gifted and talented far away; the high school freshman who is being pressured to make a decision about a college either by his parents or the colleges themselves may simply not have the maturity or the resources to come to an appropriate decision. If students are given choices beyond their capacity for decision making, they may react with avoidance, confusion, and anxiety. Often adults expect that gifted children can make difficult decisions simply because of their excellent reasoning abilities. But advanced reasoning abilities are of no help in weighing emotions. Counselors can help gifted students by giving them permission to ask others to make choices for them sometimes.

At times, however, parents and teachers are unwilling to make choices for students. In this case counselors can help by providing the gifted student with decision-making strategies that take into account both the situation as well as the student's feelings about the situation. A decision-making model such as force-counterforce analysis can be useful. In this exercise, the young person works on one decision at a time. A choice is written out as a yes or no question. For example, should I attend the Duke University summer program? Then all the forces in favor of the decision are recorded as well as all the forces against the decision. A numerical value from 1 to 10 is assigned to each force in order to indicate its strength. Therefore, the decision results not from having more reasons to support it but from the cumulative strength of forcefully held beliefs.

## Depression

Depression among gifted students is increasingly becoming a concern of parents and educators. Many of the same situations that lead to stress for the bright child can also become precursors of depression. Under conditions of prolonged stress a student may gradually lose motivation, energy, and the will to go on. In the previous section on stress and the gifted student, examples were given of students who were overextended and "burning the candle at both ends." Often the student who has not dealt with the stress of overcommitment eventually becomes depressed. Likewise students who have been forced into situations that overtax their emotional and intellectual capacity will often move from anxiety into depression. A student who converts his or her stresses and anxieties into physical symptoms such as headaches and stomachaches is still trying to succeed beyond his or her abilities; the depressed student has stopped trying. The depressed gifted student presents a challenge to the counselor precisely because intervention should have come much sooner. By the time a student is depressed because of overextension, time management and decision-making skills will not help. A 17-year-old young man came to counseling at the Counseling Laboratory for Talent Development because he felt "frozen." He said he felt paralyzed in his relationship and work, and seemed unable to feel any emotion. He had been an extremely competitive tennis, soccer, and baseball player and a straight-A student. Even his language was filled with the vocabulary of competitiveness: "She had the advantage of me when she said she liked me first" and "I think I can win out over this depression if I work at it."

This kind of depression must be treated like any form of burnout. Students like this require a moratorium from activities, a slow process of engagement with rewarding activity, and at least short-term counseling or psychotherapy in which the student can discuss his or her feelings, or lack of feelings. Often family and friends need to be brought into the process in order to help the student create a new manageable and rewarding life-style.

Cognitive behavior therapy, which replaces unrealistic beliefs with realistic beliefs, may be particularly helpful to "burned-out" gifted students. Counselors often use the lists of irrational beliefs developed by Ellis and Harper (1975). In the case just described, the counselor helped the client to see that all of life could not be conceptualized as a competition. The client learned to rethink his beliefs, to use new words to describe his experiences, and finally, to change his behavior so that he had a more relaxed, open approach to relationships and his work.

Delisle (1990) developed a list of healthy beliefs specifically for gifted students. They are as follows:

*Seven Realities for Successful Transition*
*From Adolescence to Young Adulthood*

Reality #1: Remember that the *real* basics go beyond reading, writing, and 'rithmetic.

Reality #2: You can be good at something you don't enjoy doing.

Reality #3: You can be good at some things that are unpopular among your friends.
Reality #4: Life is not a race to see who can get to the end the fastest.
Reality #5: You have the ability to ask questions which *should* have right answers, but don't.
Reality #6: It's never too late to be what you might have been.
Reality #7: A life's career is not a life sentence.

Another type of depression that seems to be almost unique to gifted students is a kind of premature existential depression (Webb et al., 1982). Existential depression occurs in gifted children and adolescents when their capacity for absorbing information about disturbing events is greater than their capacity to process and understand it. Second graders who are capable of reading news magazine accounts of war and pollution may understand the information but not be able to deal with their helplessness to do anything about it. As Leta Hollingworth (1926) pointed out long ago, many gifted children feel trapped in a world created by adults that is somehow out of control.

Gifted children's existential depression can result not only from their advanced reading ability but also from their participation in activities that call for greater maturity. One bright girl was so effective in working with animals at an animal shelter that she was given increasing amounts of veterinary responsibilities. Her work changed from simply taking wounded pets from individuals who had brought them in to preparing them for treatment, and finally to helping with the euthanasia of dogs and cats too sick or hurt to be adopted. This 12-year-old volunteer was heard to say, "I've seen too much death." Similarly, gifted teenagers who do volunteer work in hospitals and crisis centers may, because of their intelligence and skill, be given adult responsibilities without appropriate support.

Some gifted students seem to experience existential depression as a result of having wrestled with concepts with which even the wisest of adults have struggled. The meaning of life, the inevitability of death, and the beginning and end of the universe are all subjects that may lead to depression in the child or adolescent who is attempting to understand them. Perhaps the depression results from the incongruence between the child's developmental stage and intellectual abilities. A young person whose cognitive development is still "dualistic," that is, still perceiving the world in terms of absolutes such as right and wrong or good and bad, may be disturbed by reading about and thinking about questions for which there simply are no right or wrong answers. Unable to resolve the ambiguity, the student lapses into anger and despair. Perhaps one of the most helpful techniques for this kind of existential depression is bibliotherapy. Counselors can recommend books that are appropriate developmentally as well as intellectually. Stephen Schroeder-Davis (1990) developed a comprehensive, annotated list of books that are appropriate for bibliotherapy. He says that books used in bibliotherapy with the gifted should meet the following criteria:

1. They are good literature. That is, independent of their relevance to the gifted, the books are well written and fun to read. Many are by award-winning authors or have won awards themselves.
2. Giftedness is important, but not necessarily central to the story. The book must be *concerned* with the gifted, but not "about" giftedness.
3. Readers should be able to identify with the characters, themes, and conflicts. Therefore, portrayals that are rich, varied, and realistic rather than stereotyped or derogatory should be chosen.

Schroeder-Davis's selected, annotated bibliotherapy list is included in its entirety in the Resources section at the end of the book.

The book *Guiding Gifted Readers* (Halstead, 1988) provides guidelines for selecting reading as well as excellent lists of books for helping gifted students to deal with unanswerable questions. The counselor should keep in the office books that have been particularly meaningful to him or her so that these can be shared with the bright student dealing with existential concerns. There is evidence that gifted students who have been guided toward self-actualization and meaning are less likely to be depressed (Berndt, Kaiser, & Van Aalst, 1982).

## Suicide

Although the statistics have been overblown and the newspaper accounts of gifted students who have committed suicide have been overly dramatized, the fact remains that a high proportion of students who commit suicide are at least above-average students. There is not, and probably never has been, an epidemic of suicide among gifted students as the news media perhaps have intimated. However, there have been many needless deaths. Jim Delisle (1986) examined several issues surrounding adolescent suicide. He showed how gifted students, having tried all the options that they perceive to be available to them for resolving their problems may opt instead for "death with honors." Most gifted students who attempt or commit suicide do not do so purely because they are gifted, but instead because of the intensity and duration of psychological and situational problems they have been experiencing. It is not necessarily true that these stressors and situational problems of gifted students are any more severe than those experienced by average students; in fact, it may be that gifted students die more often because they are more effective planners of their own suicides. As in all cases of adolescent suicide, counselors must take any talk of suicide extremely seriously and must act promptly to prevent that event. The only difference in dealing with bright students who are suicidal is that the students may mislead counselors with their ability to articulate their problems. The counselor, having listened to the suicidal client talk about his or her problems for several hours, may feel satisfied that the problems have been dealt with and "talked through." However, it is possible for a gifted student to talk a great deal about his or her problems and still intend to commit suicide. Gifted students may engage in more deception and may be much more careful in their planning; therefore, it is dangerous to accept a student's statement that everything is fine. Every possible effort must be made to monitor the suicidal student's behavior and to restrain him or her from situations conducive to suicide. Suicidal gifted students should not be left alone, nor should they be left without a careful schedule of therapy and therapeutic activity. Institutionalization may be necessary when the student requires observation. There are many excellent guidebooks for counselors working with suicidal adolescents. Counselors need to be familiar with suicide prevention approaches.

What about the gifted adolescent who is successful in his or her suicide attempt? The suicide of a gifted student, like that of any other student, can be traumatic for an entire school. When a bright student dies, it is important that counselors stress that death is not a punishment for giftedness. Being bright does not lead to suicide. Nobody knows how the stresses of being gifted relate to depression and suicide exactly; however, the vast majority of well-adjusted gifted adolescents should provide ample evidence that extreme intelligence alone should not be a determinant of a desire to take one's life.

# Perfectionism

Very few clients are likely to refer themselves to counselors for problems with perfectionism. Instead, friends and family often pressure them into counseling out of concern or frustration with their tendency to be hard on themselves and others. Perfectionism has been described as a problem of gifted individuals by most of those who have studied them at close hand. Hollingworth (1926) saw perfectionism as a common characteristic of the highly gifted; Whitmore (1980) related it to fear of failure and underachievement; and Roedell (1987) outlined its consequences. Perfectionism here is defined as a complex of characteristics and behaviors including compulsiveness with regard to work habits, overconcern for details, unrealistically high standards for self and others, indiscriminate acquiescence to external evaluation, and rigid routines.

## Possible Causes

*Inherent Tendencies.*    Although the commonsense notion of the causes of perfectionism tends to lay the blame for the perfectionistic child squarely on "pushy," exacting parents, clinical experience shows this conclusion to be unwarranted. Many perfectionistic gifted children are the products of relaxed, easy-going parents with realistic expectations. Developmental psychologists have established that infants come into the world with tendencies to develop particular temperaments, differing among themselves on many variables such as activity level, sensitivity to change in the environment, reactivity, and mood. It seems possible that certain children are simply *born* with the combination of temperaments that create a need for an orderly environment, or conversely, an aversion to chaos. Children born with these temperaments who are also of high intelligence may be able to carry perfectionism further than average children, simply because they often have the ability to carry out tasks expected of their age level perfectly. In this way perfectionism becomes entrenched. The ability to perform perfectly combines with the need to perform perfectly (Adderholt-Elliott, 1989).

*Lack of Awareness of Giftedness.*    Many gifted children are unaware of their abilities and many have never been labeled as gifted (Webb et al., 1982). Even those who have received a label have seldom been given specific information about their abilities: How gifted? In which areas? In what percentile? How many other children can be expected to perform similarly? In the absence of specific information about how their intellectual abilities compare with those of others, gifted children and their parents usually underestimate the children's abilities or assume their intelligence to be "just average." When a child assumes that he or she is "just average," but consistently receives higher marks and consistently performs age-level tasks with ease, then that child begins to search for other explanations for his or her superiority. Children who believe their superiority is purely the result of hard work are in danger of becoming perfectionistic, just as they are in danger of becoming "elitist," as pointed out earlier.

If a gifted child assumes that his or her superiority is the result only of effort, rather than some combination of effort and ability, it is likely that the child will begin to see other children as *not* expending effort, and not living up to expectations. A child who holds other children in contempt for their lack of effort grows up to be an adult with impossibly high standards for others as well as a warped sense of his or her own capabilities.

On the other hand, a child whose gifts are identified early, and who has specific explanations of his or her abilities ("About 95 children out of 100 can't read as well as you do"; "Your math ability in 7th grade is about equal to the average 12th grader"), is likely to feel comfortable with those gifts. He or she is also more likely to have more realistic expectations of average peers, while having somewhat higher expectations of himself or herself in age-level tasks.

*Extrinsic Motivation.* Although they are more rare than believers in "the hurried child" syndrome would have it, there are parents and teachers who have made the mistake of setting up systems of rewards or punishments for every conceivable achievement or behavior. Gifted children whose abilities have been shaped by ever-increasing contingencies and who have been pressured into performing for points, grades, and awards soon lose a sense of ownership of their talents. An overemphasis on rewards can lead to less creative, more automatic behavior. A gifted child can develop perfectionistic behavior when he or she responds to *all* situations as an opportunity to gain "points." Although lacking in creativity, the work of the gifted perfectionist is always precise, correct, and full of detail in order to get the hoped-for reward. Gifted perfectionists generalize their perfectionism to relationships, hobbies, and even religion so that they seem to be trying to get an "A" in marriage, leisure, or spirituality.

## Strategies for Change

Miriam Adderholt-Elliott, in her book *Perfectionism: What's So Bad About Being Good* (1989), offered many helpful explanations for the origins of perfectionism in gifted children and ways of bringing about change. A program of behavior change for gifted perfectionists, dubbed by one of our clients "Slob for a Week," is one of my favorite techniques arising from the Guidance Laboratory for Gifted and Talented. By teaching perfectionists how to role play a "slob," the technique may help them to undo some of their more rigid behaviors; to empathize with the plight of nonperfectionists; and to learn indirectly the value of setting priorities on tasks. The Perfectionism Behavior Change Contract is included in the Resources section at the end of the book.

When guided with the right proportion of humor and seriousness, this technique can help the perfectionist to gain some new insights into his or her habits. In addition, many perfectionists learn that when they are able to give up their obsession with precision, details, and outside evaluation, they are better able to focus their energies on issues of real concern to them. One client who used the technique said, "When I gave up being perfect I rediscovered excellence in the thing I really care about—my creative writing."

Other approaches to perfectionism include rational-emotive therapy (RET) (Ellis & Harper, 1975) and Gestalt therapy (Perls et al., 1951). RET attacks the irrational belief that one must be perfect in all things at all times and replaces it with more logical beliefs. Gestalt therapy "loosens" rigid, compulsive behaviors through humorous frustrations of the client's attempts to be the "perfect client."

## Problems in Relationships

What kinds of problems in relationships are unique to gifted and talented individuals? Although gifted people experience the same societal expectations as other men and women, they do have special problems in friendships and intimate relationships that are related to their special talents. Terman and Oden (1935) found that the majority of gifted children and adolescents were well adjusted and popular with their classmates. Although the Terman subjects married later than average Americans, they tended to have very stable marriages and well-adjusted families. Hollingworth (1926) found that the great differences in intellect between highly gifted and average peers created difficulty in establishing friendships for this group. Kaufmann (1981), who also studied the highly gifted—the Presidential Scholars—found that they often received *less* recognition than their less gifted peers. She also found that Presidential Scholars married very late compared to the national average, and were virtually childless. Problems in relationships among the gifted may be related to several issues.

*Peer Relationships.*   Webb et al. (1982) reviewed the major problems gifted and talented students have in peer relationships. Many difficulties gifted students have in peer relationships relate to their uneven development. Often, gifted young people's intellectual development outstrips that of their same-age peers to the point where they become "group deviants": they are simply too different intellectually to be accepted by their age-mates. Webb et al. suggested that gifted children need several different peer groups that fit their different physical, intellectual, and social levels of development. They also pointed out that what adults consider to be satisfactory peer relationships may be very different from what the gifted child considers to be satisfactory. Pressuring gifted children to "fit in" makes them feel as if they must hide their gifts and their true selves. Too often, adults assume that a gifted child lacks social skills when the actual case is that the child *has* social skills, but chooses not to use them.

*Intimate Relationships.*   Some difficulties in intimate relationships for the gifted are simply the result of demographics. Availability of appropriate partners becomes more problematic the greater the intelligence level or the rarer the talent. In American society, men tend to marry their intellectual equals or their intellectual inferiors. As a result, there may be fewer gifted men available for gifted women. Another perspective is that if shared interests and values are an important basis of marriage, gifted men and women may have to search longer for partners who share their unusual or unique interests and possibly more intellectually oriented values.

Problems in intimate relationships for gifted people also have their roots in childhood socialization and expectations. Gifted girls, in particular, receive mixed messages about relationships. Until adolescence, they are generally rewarded primarily for achievement behaviors. As adolescence approaches, however, girls are rewarded more for their success in relationships and less for success in the classroom (Kerr, 1985). Therefore, many gifted young women become conflicted, unsure as to whether relationship goals or academic goals should be primary. Gifted young men also seem to respond to their socialization with unrealistic expectations; despite the overwhelming number of women entering and staying in the job market, a majority of gifted young men don't want their future wives to work (Fox, 1976)! Male-female stereotypes, which are harmful to people in general, may be very harmful to gifted young men and women, whose dreams for themselves and whose needs in relationships don't conform to social norms for men and women.

Finally, gifted people experience problems in relationships when they generalize achievement-oriented behavior to relationships. That is, when a gifted individual evaluates and selects partners in terms of which one will seem to others to be the greatest achievement, problems result. Individuals who generalize achievement-oriented behaviors need help in learning to separate accomplishment from intimacy.

Webb et al. (1982) and Kerr (1985) provided a number of suggestions for strategies for guiding gifted young people in the area of relationships. At the Counseling Laboratory for Talent Development, the Role-Stripping exercise was modified to help gifted students examine the roles and relationships that hold the greatest significance for them. By setting priorities to their roles, and processing the results, gifted students are able to explore the meaning of their relationships and to receive counseling with regard to conflicts. Instructions for Role Stripping are included in the Resources section at the end of the book.

## Summary

This chapter dealt with the major adjustment concerns of gifted and talented students. It must be remembered, however, that gifted individuals encounter all the psychological disorders experienced by the general population. Whether the incidence of psychological adjustment problems is higher or lower among the gifted than among the general population is still a subject of much debate. Nevertheless, common problems such as depression and anxiety among gifted clients should never be considered separately from giftedness. It is often said that a child is a child first, and then gifted; but this misses the mark in that intellectual giftedness and its attendant isolation and stresses are so often part of the problem. Delisle (1986) showed the dangers of ignoring the stresses of giftedness in his essay on suicide and the gifted. Therefore, the counselor who wishes to help the gifted must first make a sincere effort to understand the special characteristics of that population. He or she must be willing to try creative strategies for intervening in the concerns of gifted young people. An understanding of the needs of the gifted and talented throughout the life span, together with a readiness to synthesize new approaches, makes it possible to help bright young people fulfill their promise.

## References

Adderholt-Elliott, M. (1989). *Perfectionism: What's so bad about being good.* Minneapolis, MN: Free Spirit.

Berndt, D. J., Kaiser, C. F., & Van Aalst, F. (1982). Depression and self-actualization in gifted adolescents. *Journal of Clinical Psychology, 38,* 142–150.

Bloom, B. S. (1985). *Developing talent in young people.* New York: Ballantine Books.

Brody, L. E., & Benbow, C. P. (1986). Social and emotional adjustment of adolescents extremely talented in verbal or mathematical reasoning. *Journal of Youth and Adolescence, 15,* 1–18.

Buescher, T. M. (Ed.) (1987). *Understanding gifted and talented adolescents: A resource guide.* Evanston, IL: Center for Talent Development.

Delisle, J. R. (1984). *Gifted children speak out.* New York: Walker.

Delisle, J. R. (1986). Death with honors: Suicide among gifted adolescents. Special Issue: Counseling Gifted and Talented. *Journal of Counseling and Development, 64,* 558–560.

Delisle, J. R. (1990, April). *Working with gifted adolescents.* Paper presented at national convention of the Council for Exceptional Children, Toronto.

Ellis, A., & Harper, R. A. (1975). *A new guide to rational living.* New York: Institute for Rational Living.

Fox, L. H. (1976). *Changing behaviors and attitudes of gifted girls.* Paper presented at the annual convention of the American Psychological Association, Washington, DC.

Frederickson, R. H., & Rothney, J. W. M. (1972). *Recognizing and assisting multipotential youth.* Columbus, OH: Merrill.

Gardner, H. (1983). *Frames of mind: The theory of multiple intelligences.* New York, NY: Basic Books.

Gottfredson, G. D., & Holland, J. L. (1989). *Dictionary of Holland occupational codes.* New York: Psychological Assessments Resources.

Groth, N. J. (1969). *Vocational development for gifted girls.* (ERIC Document Reproduction Service, ED 931747)

Haier, R. J., & Denham, S. A. (1976). A summary profile of nonintellectual correlates of mathematical precocity in boys and girls. In P. Keating (Ed.), *Intellectual talent: Research and development* (pp. 224–235). Baltimore: Johns Hopkins University Press.

Halstead, J. W. (1988). *Guiding gifted readers.* Columbus, OH: Ohio Psychology.

Hollinger, C. L., & Fleming, E. S. (1985). Social orientation and the social self-esteem of gifted and talented female adolescents. *Journal of Youth and Adolescence, 14,* 389–399.

Hollingworth, L. S. (1926). *Gifted children: Their nature and nurture.* New York: Macmillan.

Hollingworth, L. S. (1942). *Children over 180 IQ Stanford Binet: Origin and development.* Yonkers, NY: World Book.

Janos, P. M., & Robinson, N. M. (1985). Psychosocial development in intellectually gifted children. In F. D. Horowitz and M. O'Brien (Eds.), *The gifted and talented: Developmental perspectives.* Washington, DC: American Psychological Association.

Kaiser, C. F., & Berndt, D. J. (1985). Predictors of loneliness in the gifted adolescent. *Gifted Child Quarterly, 29,* 74–77.

Karnes, F. A., & Wherry, J. N. (1983). CPQ personality factors of upper elementary gifted students. *Journal of Personality Assessment, 47,* 303–304.

Kaufmann, F. (1981). The 1964–1968 Presidential Scholars: A follow-up study. *Exceptional Children, 48,* 2.

Kelly, K., & Colangelo, N. (1990). Effects of academic ability and gender on career development. *Journal for the Education of the Gifted, 13,* 168–175.

Kerr, B. A. (1982). *Career education for the gifted and talented.* Columbus, OH: ERIC Clearinghouse on Adult, Career, and Vocational Education.

Kerr, B. A. (1985). *Smart girls, gifted women.* Columbus, OH: Ohio Psychology.

Kerr, B. A., Colangelo, N., & Gaeth, J. (1987). Gifted adolescents' attitudes toward their giftedness. *Gifted Child Quarterly, 32*(2), 245–248.

Kerr, B. A., Hallowell, K., & Erb, C. B. (1989, November). *Adjustment of students with specific extraordinary talents.* Paper presented at the National Association for Gifted Children, New Orleans, LA.

Kulik, J. A., & Kulik, C. C. (1983). Effects of accelerated instruction of students. *Review of Educational Research*, *54*, 409–425.

Lehman, E. G., & Erdwins, C. J. (1981). The social and emotional adjustment of young, intellectually gifted children. *Gifted Child Quarterly*, *25*, 134–137.

Moreno, J. R. (1946–1969). *Psychodrama* (Vol. 1–3). Beacon, NJ: Beacon Press.

Perls, F., Hefferline, R. F., & Goodman, P. (1951). *Gestalt therapy*. New York: Julian Press.

Roedell, W. (1987). Vulnerabilities of highly gifted children. *Roeper Review*, *6*(3), 127–129.

Schroeder-Davis, S. (1990). *Affirming giftedness through fiction*. Unpublished dissertation, College of St. Thomas, St. Paul, MN.

Terman L. M., & Oden, M. H. (1935). *The promise of youth*. Genetic studies of genius, 3. Stanford, CA: Stanford University Press.

Terman, L. M., & Oden, M. H. (1947). The gifted child grows up. *Genetic Studies of Genius*, *4*. Stanford, CA: Stanford University Press.

Webb, J. T., Meckstroth, E. A., & Tolan, S. S. (1982). *Guiding the gifted child*. Columbus, OH: Ohio Psychology.

Whitmore, J. (1980). *Giftedness, conflict, and underachievement*. Boston, MA: Allyn & Bacon.

Yadusky-Holahan, M., & Holahan, W. (1983). The effect of academic stress upon anxiety and depression levels of gifted high school students. *Gifted Child Quarterly*, *27*, 42–46.

In the previous chapters, suggestions for identifying gifted students, providing career counseling, providing academic guidance, and dealing with specific psychological adjustment problems were presented. Many techniques and strategies are useful across all kinds of counseling with gifted students. In a way, many techniques presented here are actually just the manifestations of positive, helpful attitudes toward gifted and talented students.

These suggestions for counseling gifted students are based on the experiences of counselors at the Guidance Laboratory for Gifted and Talented at the University of Nebraska and the Counseling Laboratory for Talent Development at The University of Iowa. They are grouped into two categories: designing guidance services for the gifted and talented, and counseling techniques.

# Counseling Gifted Students: Techniques That Work

## Designing Guidance Services

Although it is probably not necessary that gifted students have a separate, specialized counseling service, it may be useful for the counselor to have a different system for keeping records and providing services to gifted students. Having a system of records and a plan for counseling gifted students ensures that gifted students' needs will not be overlooked in the course of trying to provide a wide variety of services to a diverse student group. Sometimes a school already has an individualized approach to guidance that emphasizes the talent development of each student; a system like this can be easily modified to provide for the special needs of gifted students. Some suggestions for structuring guidance services to gifted and talented students follow.

1. The file of every gifted and talented student should contain the transcripts of that student's coursework; a clear description of the student's special talents; a description of all results from ability tests that have been administered to that student by the counselor, school psychologist, or a private psychologist; any interest, personality, or values inventory results that may exist for that student; a record of summer school attendance and attendance at special camps and institutes for the gifted and talented; a description of out-of-class accomplishments, particularly awards, recognitions, and outstanding products; and a goal-setting sheet similar to the one described in chapter 5 on Career Planning in which a student has outlined two or three goals and his or her plans for attaining those goals.

2. If an assessment program does not already exist in the school, the counselor may wish to develop his or her own psychological assessment system for gifted students. Psychological assessment may consist of additional tests of intellectual abilities and aptitudes that the counselor is qualified to give; vocational interest tests; personality tests with which the counselor is familiar and competent; and values inventories.

3. The counselor should keep a library of materials likely to be of particular interest to gifted and talented students. Career education materials should include biographies such as those listed in the Resources section for gifted girls, materials for career counseling, as well as career education and college planning materials specially designed for gifted students. I referred to many of these materials in chapter 6 on counseling gifted girls, chapter 5 on career counseling, and chapter 4 on college planning. Also in the counselor's library should be a copy (or multiple copies) of favorite books for bibliotherapy.

4. Counselors can design a guidance plan for each gifted student that focuses on the development of talent. Each academic year the counselor should meet with the student alone several times, and at least once with parents to plan for the academic year ahead. Individual sessions with the

gifted student alone can be devoted to developmental counseling focusing on the student's adjustment and achievement of his or her own goals. Sessions with parents can evaluate the overall impact of curriculum and special activities on the student's development, and also can be informational sessions about future opportunities and goals.

5. For the counselor with a large caseload of gifted and talented students, group guidance is not only an efficient way of providing registration, but also an opportunity for gifted students to interact with one another in planning for the future and discussing current issues in their lives. Group guidance with the gifted and talented can be organized around topics covered in this handbook. Group sessions might include a workshop on adjustment and self-esteem; a workshop on sex roles, relationships, and giftedness; a career planning workshop; and a college planning seminar.

6. The counselor should work closely with the gifted coordinator and with teachers of gifted students in developing a consultative relationship. The gifted education coordinator and other teachers need to be aware of the counselor's special expertise. In addition, the counselor can learn from the gifted educator and teachers more about the characteristics and needs of his or her gifted clients. Too often consulting remains on an informal basis and busy schedules overwhelm the good intentions of all parties to meet. Therefore the counselor might want to set up, at the beginning of each year, at least one formal meeting with the teachers of the gifted and perhaps the gifted student representative in order to develop a plan to meet the needs of gifted students.

## Techniques for Counseling the Gifted and Talented

Most of the techniques for counseling gifted and talented students are simply the techniques all good counselors use: listening skills, persuasion skills, and behavior change skills. The following techniques are really attitudes and behaviors that can help the counselor to be more effective with intellectually able students and students with specific extraordinary talents (Kerr, 1990).

1. Counseling with gifted students must be child-centered, as Hollingworth (1926) first demonstrated. The more remarkable the gifts of

Adapted from Kerr, B. A. (1990). Leta Hollingworth's Legacy to Counseling and Guidance. *Roeper Review, 12*(3), 178–181.

the bright student, the greater is the investment that individuals have in the decisions that student makes. In the life of every gifted student there are teachers, parents, administrators, and friends with strong opinions about that child. In addition, there is often a great deal of information available in the records from former teachers and counselors. Despite the involvement of parents and teachers and despite the documents and records that exist, the counselor's first duty is to receive the gifted child's description of the problem or concerns in the child's own words. The child must be the focus of the counseling and therapy process. Sometimes in our rush to develop a child's talent we forget the child's own feelings and beliefs about his or her gifts. Only by understanding the child's giftedness from within the child's frame of reference can the counselor help to develop the child's gifts to their full potential.

2. In understanding the psychology of the gifted child, intellectual abilities as well as personality characteristics must be taken into account. Many counselors of gifted students have observed that gifts seem to have a life of their own. For example, verbal precocity is a hunger for reading, writing, and expression that the individual cannot ignore. Mathematical precocity has an insistence of its own, demanding that the student go further and deeper into an understanding of math. Almost every talent carries with it its own drive and appetite for actualization. Therefore, to attempt to counsel the child without guiding the gift is to misunderstand the nature of the gifted child. It is often said that the gifted child is a child first, and then gifted. However, this statement may be misleading. A gifted child cannot be understood apart from his or her gifts.

3. A counselor's attitude toward a gifted student should be positive, constructive, and comfortable. As Hollingworth (1926) noted long ago, professionals who work with gifted students often feel threatened or are overly admiring. Neither of these attitudes is helpful. The counselor who feels threatened by the gifted child may feel tempted to test the child's knowledge, as if to make the child prove that he or she is gifted. The counselor who is threatened may avoid gifted students, not wanting students to know about his or her lack of experience.

The counselor who is overly admiring may be equally harmful. The awestruck counselor may feel overwhelmed by the verbally brilliant student's conversational abilities, allowing the counseling session to be sidetracked. Instead of being frightened or dazzled, probably the best attitude to strive for is one of friendly helpfulness and positive challenge. A counselor can be an empathic listener as well as a mentor who expects excellence from the student.

4. A counselor should always show curiosity rather than ignorance or indifference. For better or worse, many gifted students base their opinions of others on their perceptions of others' intellectual interests and abilities. In order for counselors to be effective and influential with their gifted students, it is necessary that their students perceive them as intelligent people with lively interests in the kinds of intellectual endeavors in which the students are interested. This does not mean that the counselor has to be an expert on such things as Fermat's theorem, Dylan Thomas's poetry, or the language of dolphins. Instead, it means that when students discuss these kinds of subjects the counselor should show a lively curiosity and willingness to learn about the topics that are exciting to the students. The basic techniques of good attending behaviors are exactly those that enable the counselor to show curiosity and interest. When a student remarks that she or he is interested in developing software for playing Dungeons and Dragons, the counselor can simply respond with, "That sounds fascinating! Tell me more about it." Or "What is it about developing software for games that excites you?" The counselor will learn a lot of interesting facts in these kinds of conversations, and gifted students will perceive the counselor as credible and persuasive.

5. The counseling process with gifted students often points up the necessity for change not only in the student but in the family, the school, and society. Many problems gifted students present to the counselor are not really their own problems but rather problems of the system in which they are trying to learn and grow. To help a gifted child to cope with the boredom of being in the regular classroom, the counselor must do more than help the student with coping skills. Instead, the counselor must act as an advocate for that student, helping the student to achieve a more challenging curriculum. To help the student who is experiencing extraordinary stress from academic pressure, the counselor must work with parents and students together to create a healthier attitude toward achievement.

Often, if the counselor is to do a good job as a helper to gifted students, he or she must become involved in action for change in the school system and in society. Many counselors who are experienced in working with gifted students enjoy the opportunity to meet other counselors of the gifted at state and national professional organizations that work for the betterment of gifted students. Counselors also can help empower gifted students to bring about changes themselves. By teaching their gifted students communication and persuasion skills, counselors may be able to help them to influence teachers and administrators to provide the kind of education they need.

## Summary

At the beginning of this book, I said that those counselors who decide to guide gifted students are taking on a challenging but rewarding task. I have reviewed the challenges to the counselor in providing for the psychological adjustment, career planning, and academic guidance of the gifted student. The rewards of counseling the gifted student are much more difficult to describe; in fact they must be experienced. Perhaps the best way to describe the experience of counseling gifted students is to liken it to cutting diamonds. Like the jeweler who cuts precious gems, the counselor to the gifted gently guides and shapes the student's abilities and interests so that the brilliance might shine through.

## References

Hollingworth, L. S. (1926). *Gifted children: Their nature and nurture.* New York: Macmillan.
Kerr, B. A. (1990). Leta Hollingworth's legacy to counseling and guidance. *Roeper Review, 12*(3), 178–181.

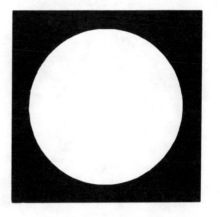

# *Resources*

# 1

## Resources

___

# Standardized Instruments Used in Identification of Gifted Students

### Wechsler Intelligence Scale for Children-Revised

The WISC-R is the most widely used intelligence test and is truly useful. It is an individually administered test for children aged 6 to 16. The WISC-R has up to 15 possible subscales that yield a performance score, a verbal score, and a total score. The tests that make up the verbal score include the following: information, comprehension, arithmetic, similarities, vocabulary, and the optional digit-span test. The performance tests include picture completion, picture arrangement, block design, object assembly, coding, and the optional mazes. Each test is easily and rapidly administered.

It is interesting to note that the WISC-R is *not* based on a theory of intelligence. Instead, all the tests are derived from tradition—that is, they are tests that psychologists in the early part of this century believed to be indicative of major intellectual abilities. Over the years, however, the vast amount of research on the WISC-R has made it one of the most thoroughly evaluated psychological tests existing. The WISC-R has proven to be an excellent predictor of the ability to learn in school, and it is highly correlated with achievement tests, aptitude tests, and just about every other measure of general intellectual abilities.

The WISC-R is more than a predictor of learning ability, however; it is also an excellent instrument for generating hypotheses about the nature of a particular child's abilities as well as possible barriers to achievement. Performance on arithmetic and coding, for example, may give some notion of a child's powers of concentration; performance on comprehension may indicate the extent of a child's reasoning and judgment capabilities. A skillful interpreter not only looks at the subtest scores, but at the whole of the child's behaviors in the testing situation.

Who should administer the WISC-R? Preferably, school psychologists or other psychologists trained in individual intelligence testing should administer and interpret the WISC-R. This is not only to ensure that the test is given properly. More importantly, psychologists who are trained in the WISC-R administration also understand the psychometric and statistical properties of the test—and therefore its limitations. The danger of the administration of the WISC-R by a clerk or assistant is that the interpretation of the scores will be "mechanical," that is, based on a strict interpretation of the manual.

## Use of the WISC-R With Gifted Students

There is strong evidence that gifted students not only score higher than average individuals on the WISC-R, but that they have qualitatively different patterns of scores (Brown & Yakimowski, 1987). This may be because gifted children actually process information differently than average children. Gifted children may also vary more in their scoring patterns. Therefore, the use of a single WISC-R score to describe a gifted child's abilities may obscure more than it enlightens.

An examination of subscale scores, although considered inappropriate for average students, may be necessary to obtain a fuller understanding of the gifted child's abilities. Hollinger and Kosek (1986) argued persuasively that educators should go beyond the use of the full-scale IQ score. Their research showed great variability in performance on the subscales among students scoring higher than 130 on the full scale. About 35% of these students had significant discrepancies between their Verbal and Performance scores. Interpreting the Verbal and Performance scores separately and examining subtest scores thoroughly may ensure more effective placement in academic programs.

## The Stanford-Binet (3rd and 4th Editions)

The Stanford-Binet, developed by Lewis Terman, the "father of the gifted child movement," is traditionally considered the best instrument for identifying gifted children. Up through the 3rd edition—"Form L-M"—the Stanford-Binet was very consistent from revision to revision. The items were for the most part very similar to the original items considered by Binet, and then Terman, to be indicative of intelligence. Beginning at age 2 and proceeding through levels of Superior Adult, items include vocabulary, reasoning problems, memory of strings of digits, and general information. The 4th edition, called SB4, represents the most extensive change of format to date, although many items are the traditional ones. Because it is a recent revision, its use with gifted students has not yet been fully explored. Therefore, the 3rd edition—which is still available and widely used—and the 4th edition will be reviewed separately.

## *The Stanford-Binet (3rd Edition)*

This edition of the Stanford-Binet, developed in 1960 and renormed in 1972, is known as Form L-M because it combines two forms, L and M, developed in 1937. This widely used intelligence test yields one global score as a measure of general intellectual ability. The Stanford-Binet 3rd edition, like its predecessors, groups items according to age levels. The test taker progresses through the age levels until all the items in an age level become too difficult. This procedure yields a "mental age"; in previous editions, IQ was figured as a ratio of chronological age to mental age. The 3rd edition, however, provides a means for figuring a "deviation IQ" score, now a more commonly understood score, with a mean of 100 and a standard deviation of 16. The Stanford-Binet 3rd edition is a largely verbal test, although it does contain some nonverbal items. For gifted children, it has a very high "ceiling"—that is, even the brightest children are not likely to be able to answer all the items in the Superior Adult levels. However, for quite a few brilliant adults, the Superior Adult levels may be too easy.

## The Stanford-Binet (4th Edition)

The SB4 is a new test in several ways. First, the items are not grouped by age, but in separate tests in increasing order of difficulty. Also, for the first time, four major cognitive areas are represented, rather than one single, global entity called intelligence. The four areas are Verbal Reasoning, Quantitative Reasoning, Abstract/Visual Reasoning, and Short-Term Memory. Instead of beginning at a particular age level, an entry level is based on performance on the Vocabulary test. Then the test taker proceeds to take 8 to 13 of the 15 available tests. Each test yields a Standard Age Score (SAS) with a mean of 50 and a standard deviation of 8, which represent the individual's performance on that test compared to his or her age group. SASs are also computed for each cognitive area and for a composite; these have a mean of 100 and a standard deviation of 16. Many items are taken from old revisions, but new items have been created to test fully the four cognitive areas. Like the WISC-R, the Stanford-Binet requires a trained administrator.

## Use of the 3rd and 4th Editions With Gifted Students

The 3rd edition of the Stanford-Binet is heavily verbal in nature, but the 4th edition is less so. Nevertheless, with vocabulary as the screening test, and with vocabulary still having the strongest relationship to the general ability score, it is still a language-oriented test. Both the 3rd and 4th editions tend to yield higher intelligence scores than the WISC-R or the Kaufman ABC for gifted students. Both editions seem to provide excellent measures of gifted students' general cognitive ability. The 3rd edition is well established as a predictor of academic performance for gifted students, and the 4th edition is in the process of being established as a predictor of academic success for this group of students.

## The Kaufman Assessment Battery for Children

The K-ABC is a more recently developed intelligence test (Kaufman & Kaufman, 1983). It is a more nonverbal test than either the WISC-R or the Stanford-Binet; in fact, a completely nonverbal scale is available for hearing impaired, speech- and language-disordered, and non-English-speaking subjects. The test is for children 2.5 to 12.5 years old. It has 16 subtests, although a particular test taker would be administered a maximum of 13. The subtests are divided into 10 "mental processing" tests such as Magic Window, Face Recognition, Hand Movements, Number Recall, and Spatial Memory, and six "achievement" tests such as Expressive Vocabulary, Faces and Places, Arithmetic, and Riddles.

The distinction between "mental processing," considered to be synonymous with intelligence, and achievement is not clear; it is hard to see how some items represent native ability and others learned ability. The mental processing items are highly spatial-visual, therefore students with strong skills in these areas are likely to be rated as more intelligent than more verbally oriented students with lower spatial-visual skills.

## Use of the K-ABC With Gifted Students

The K-ABC tends to give lower estimates of intelligence for gifted students than the Stanford-Binet or WISC-R; in one study, gifted students' scores on the K-ABC were, on the average, 8 points lower than Stanford-Binet scores. However, spatially-visually gifted students with poorer English or lower verbal abilities would be favored by this test.

## Other Tests of Intellectual Ability

## The Woodcock-Johnson Psycho-Educational Battery

The Woodcock-Johnson is a set of innovative tests that measure cognitive ability, achievement, and academic interests. It can be administered to individuals aged 3 through 80. All tests have been standardized on the same norming sample. The cognitive ability test is excellent in that many items are learning tasks; the administrator can observe how the individual actually learns. The cognitive ability test includes such items as picture vocabulary, memory for sentences, analysis and synthesis, and analogue. Achievement includes such items as word attack, calculation, proofing, science, and humanities. Academic interests include reading interest, math interest, language interest, physical interest, and social interest. The flaws of the Woodcock-Johnson include complicated scoring and interpretation, and some overlap or confusion of cognitive ability and achievement items. The Woodcock-Johnson has not been used enough with gifted students to determine how students labeled as gifted perform compared to average students, or to discover how they score on this test relative to other intelligence tests. It seems, however, to be a promising instrument for this group.

## Raven Progressive Matrices

The Raven Progressive Matrices are a series of matrices in which one part is missing; the test taker has to choose, from among six alternatives, the part that best completes the matrix. This is a completely nonverbal test; the instructions can be pantomimed. The Raven Progressive Matrices correlate highly with the performance section of the WISC-R and moderately with the full-scale score. Because of its nonverbal nature, it is considered an appropriate test for non-English-speaking or language-disabled individuals, and it may hold promise as an instrument for identifying minority and disadvantaged gifted students. The Raven Progressive Matrices were very successful in identifying large numbers of minority gifted students in the Chicago public schools (Baska, 1986). The Raven is available as three scales—Colored, Standard, and Advanced (Colored does not refer to race). The Advanced Progressive Matrices seem to be the most useful with gifted students because of the high "ceiling" for this scale.

## System of Multicultural Pluralistic Assessment (SOMPA)

SOMPA is actually a test that combines WISC-R scales with rating forms in a way that provides a less biased estimate of the abilities of minority students. The SOMPA compares minority students not with mainly White, middle-class norms, but with other students within the same minority group. Therefore, Blacks are compared with Blacks, Hispanics with Hispanics, and Native Americans with Native Americans. SOMPA is a good technique for identifying gifted students within a school or district, but does not allow for comparisons across gifted programs.

## Structure of Intellect-Learning Abilities (SOI-LA) (Screening Form for the Gifted)

The SOI-LA began with structure of intellect analyses of the Stanford-Binet and the WISC to identify dimensions of giftedness. The Structure of Intellect Model holds that giftedness is multidimensional. According to Guilford, who developed the Structure of Intellect Model based on factor analyses of intelligence tests, intelligence can best be understood as a composite of 120 separate abilities. These abilities are categorized by their contents, operations, and products. Of these many abilities, the Learning Abilities Test (SOI-LA) measures 24 abilities; the Screening Form for the Gifted reduces these to 10, which yield the best results for students identified as gifted.

The SOI-LA SFG is meant to identify intellectual strengths and weaknesses of gifted students so that educational programming can be individualized. Unfortunately, the SOI-LA SFG has not performed as well as expected. According to Clarizio and Mehrens (1985), the test "promises more than it delivers" (p. 113) in that it has serious psychometric limitations. It has not yet proven to be as valid or reliable as instruments for identification need to be, and also suffers from the conceptual limitation of breaking down intellectual abilities into too many factors of too little importance. However, because the instrument may be less biased in the selection of minority and disadvantaged gifted, research needs to continue even though the scale is probably not ready for general use.

## Torrance Tests of Creative Thinking (TTCT)

The TTCT includes two tests, one verbal and one figural. The verbal test, "Thinking Creatively with Words," provides scores for fluency, flexibility, and originality. Subtests of the verbal test include Asking, Guessing Causes, Guessing Consequences, Product Improvement, Unusual Uses, Unusual Questions, and Just Suppose. The figural test, "Thinking Creatively with Pictures," provides scores for fluency, flexibility, originality, and elaboration. Subtests of the figural test include Picture Construction, Picture Completions, and Parallel Lines.

The TTCT can be administered and scored by teachers, and interrater reliabilities are high. Other forms of reliability are moderate; overall, the test is well constructed. A major problem with the TTCT is determining what it really tests, because there is no well-explained theory of creativity behind the tests. It is not clear what the relationship of fluency, flexibility, originality, and elaboration is to actual, productive creativity. Also, there is considerable overlap among fluency, flexibility, and originality; a single total score might be more appropriate. Torrance never claimed this to be a definitive test of creativity, or that it should be used alone to identify creative giftedness. Rather, the TTCT is best used as a research instrument or to support other observations and tests. It is an interesting, enjoyable test for test takers; however, the scoring for the test administrator is tedious.

## Achievement Tests

### Stanford Achievement Test (1982)

Six levels of this test are available, ranging from grades 1.5–2.9 to grades 7.0–9.9. Subtests in mathematics, reading, and listening comprehension are available as separates. Partial batteries are available without science and social science subjects (grades 3.5–9.9). An optional writing assessment program is available (grades 3.5 - 9.9). This is one of the best available achievement batteries. This edition is part of an outstanding tradition of item writing, item analysis, content analysis, and norming.

### Peabody Individual Achievement Test (PIAT; 1970)

This test may be administered to grades K-12. It yields six scores: mathematics, reading recognition, reading comprehension, spelling, general information, and total. It is designed to be administered to individuals.

### Wide Range Achievement Test (WRAT; 1978)

The WRAT has two levels: ages 5–11 and ages 12–64. It provides three scores: spelling, arithmetic, and reading. A tape cassette is available for ease of administration. The WRAT has adequate technical qualities, but overall is not an adequate diagnostic instrument for the gifted and talented.

## References

Baska, L. (1986). Alternatives to traditional testing. *Roeper Review, 8*(3), 181–184.

Brown, S. W., & Yakimowski, M. E. (1987). Intelligence scores of gifted students on the WISC-R. *Gifted Child Quarterly, 31*(3), 130–134.

Clarizio, H. F., & Mehrens, W. A. (1985). Psychometric limitation of Guilford's structure-of-intellect model for identification and programming of the gifted. *Gifted Child Quarterly, 29*(3), 113–120.

Hollinger, C. L., & Kosek, S. (1986). Beyond the use of full scale I.Q. scores. *Gifted Child Quarterly, 30*(2), 74–77.

Kaufman, A. S., & Kaufman, N. L. (1983). *Kaufman Assessment Battery for Children.* Circle Pines, MN: American Guidance System.

# Resources

## Program Design Standards of the Council for Exceptional Children— The Association for the Gifted*

Program design is the plan for the administrative configuration through which instruction is delivered to gifted and talented students. Since these students are receiving service throughout the educational system, programs that fall into this category go beyond those designated as "G/T" and include *all* programs in which gifted and talented students are involved. The intent is to build a flexible system of viable program options throughout the general and special education structures that are compatible with and can be matched to the strengths, needs, and interests of gifted and talented students.

### 1. Programs for the Gifted and Talented Are Articulated With General Education Programs

Programs for the gifted and talented are part of the general program offerings of the school district, as these students are typically involved in programs that are considered general education.

* Reprinted from Council for Exceptional Children—The Association for the Gifted. (1990). *Standards for Program Involving the Gifted and Talented*. Reston, VA: ERIC Clearinghouse on Handicapped and Gifted Children.

Articulation involves planning the extension of general education programs in order to address the needs of these students; policy review to assure that policies encourage involvement in rigorous programs; and communication between parties to keep all participants informed and the program developing.

## 2. Programs Are Comprehensive, Structured, and Sequenced Across Grade Levels

Comprehensive programs for the gifted and talented go beyond academics and include options in areas such as the arts, leadership, and creativity. These programs are planned and ordered so that students can continue to develop their skills.

## 3. Programs Are an Integral Part of the School Day and May Be Extended to Other School and Community Related Settings

Programs for the gifted and talented are central to the students' educational program and meet during the school day. In some instances, programs may be held before or after school or in settings other than school when the nature of the experience (not the convenience of the schedule) requires this timing.

## 4. Administrative Structures and Program Options Are Based on Student Needs

The program options offered are determined by the needs of the students being served. These options may vary based on the needs and resources of the community. Ongoing needs assessments are necessary in order to assure that current needs and options are compatible.

## 5. All Gifted and Talented Students Are Assured Programs Commensurate With Their Abilities

Programs are available that represent the varying ranges of ability and needs displayed by gifted and talented students. Access to the programs is guaranteed to these students.

## 6. Resources for Program Development and Implementation Are Distributed Equitably Throughout the School District

Gifted and talented students throughout a school district are given appropriate educational programs regardless of the school they attend. Resources are distributed based on student needs.

## 7. Programs Incorporate a Blend of Community Resources and School-Based Support Services in Program Development and Delivery

School psychologists, social workers, content area specialists, counselors, and community members add expertise to the planning and implementation of program options. They expand the range of support for the programs and open doors to opportunities for students beyond those available through the district or individual program personnel.

## 8. Specialists in Gifted Child Education Are Consulted in Program Policy Development

Informed advocates for these students give district personnel guidance in program planning so that the procedures and policies are consistent with the needs of gifted and talented students.

## 9. Ongoing Program Evaluation Activities Are Conducted for the Purpose of Continued Program Development

A plan for evaluation is in place and implemented so that program decisions are based on data generated from program students and personnel.

### Curriculum Design Standards

Curriculum design is the plan for the instructional component of the gifted and talented student's program. It includes the content, methodology, resources, and products of instruction. Without sound curricular practices, program configurations are meaningless. Curriculum involving gifted and talented students is the focus of these standards. They should be applied to any class in which gifted and talented students are enrolled.

## 1. Curriculum (Preschool-12) Is Articulated, Comprehensive, and Includes Substantive Scope and Sequence

Curriculum that responds to the needs of gifted and talented students appears in all grades and all subject areas. A scope and sequence plan outlining the types and progression of skills to be learned is available and consulted when making curricular decisions about individual students.

## 2. Curriculum Is Based on the Assessed Needs of Students Including the Areas of Intellectual, Emotional, Physical, Ethical, and Social Development

The needs of gifted and talented students extend beyond academics. Full-scale assessment conducted during or after identification can give instructors valuable information for curricular planning. A student's instructional plan reflects the unique needs of the individual student.

## 3. Curriculum Matches Substantive Content With the Developmental Levels of the Gifted and Talented Student

Most gifted students have developmental patterns that must be taken into account when planning curriculum. Physical, cognitive, and emotional growth are among the developmental factors that can affect how students learn and how they express what they have learned.

## 4. Curriculum Incorporates Content and Experiences That Employ and Facilitate Understanding of the Latest Ideas, Principles, and Technology in a Given Content Area

With rapidly changing academic fields of study, it is important that curriculum including gifted and talented students recognizes new ideas and is modified to reflect the changes in the form of the disciplines, how the fields are thought about and conveyed, what is important to know, and the technology used.

## 5. Curriculum Provides Differentiation and Challenge for Students Through Involvement With Advanced and Rigorous Content and Procedures

The content and procedures used in curriculum are compatible with the abilities of the students involved in it. The opportunity to study content at a level commensurate with ability and achievement levels is offered to all gifted and talented students.

## 6. Students Develop Critical and Creative Thinking Skills Through Instruction and Experiences Rooted in the Content Areas

Skills for processing and evaluating information are part of the curriculum design. Students employ such techniques as original research, independent study, problem solving, and invention as part of their study of content areas in order to develop these skills.

## 7. Students Have Opportunities to Engage in Experiential and Interactive Learning Involving Real Life Experiences That May Result in the Development of Sophisticated Products

Gifted and talented students are given the chance to become actively involved with the field they are studying. This may include activities such as working with a professional in the field through a mentorship or internship, studying a topic in depth in the library or laboratory, or developing an original product (i.e., book, idea, plan, portfolio, etc.) and presenting it publicly.

## 8. Flexible Pacing Is Employed, Allowing Students to Learn at the Pace and Level Appropriate to Their Abilities and Skills

Students are given the opportunity to work at their own level and pace. Assessment of skill levels, acceleration, skill groups, curriculum compacting, and individualization are among the methods that may be a part of the flexible pacing process.

## 9. Curriculum Addresses the Attitudes and Skills Needed for Lifelong Independent Learning

Gifted and talented students learn a great deal on their own. It is vital that they be given the opportunity to develop the skills needed to become lifelong, independent learners.

## 10. Specialists in Content Areas, Instructional Techniques, and Gifted Child Education Work With Curriculum Planners When Curriculum Is Being Planned and Evaluated

A team approach to curriculum planning is in place, to ensure that the curriculum responds to the needs of gifted students, reflects current content of practices in the academic fields, and is consistent with the goals and policies of the school district.

# Publications for Academic Guidance

1. *Educational Opportunities Guide*
   A Directory of Programs for the Gifted Talent Identification Program (TIP)
   Duke University
   01 West Duke Building
   Durham, NC 27708
   (919)684–3847 (Summer Residential Talent Search Office)
   (919)683–1400 (Executive Director: Dr. Robert Sawyer)

2. *Explorations: Make the Most Out of Summer!*
   Cindy Ware, Director
   30 Alcott Street
   P.O. Box 2254
   Acton, MA 01720
   (508)263–8921
   Minidirectories listed in the manual have been converted into one major volume called *Summer Options forTeenagers.*

3. *Summer on Campus: College Experiences for High School Students*
   Shirley Levin
   Published by College Entrance Examination Board
   College Board Publications
   Dept. J45, P.O. Box 886
   New York, NY 10101
   (212)713–8000

4. Teenager's Guide to Study, Travel, and Adventure Abroad
   Council on International Educational Exchange
   205 East 42nd St.
   New York, NY 10017
   (212)661-1414

5. Summer Opportunities for Kids and Teenagers
   Editor: C. Billy
   Publised by Peterson's Guides
   P.O. Box 2123
   Princeton, NJ 08543-2123
   (609)243-9111

# Resources

## An Intervention for Underachievers

Recent literature suggests that the failure of many academically talented students, particularly women, to meet their potential is a result of their inability to commit themselves to a goal or dream. This model of intervention is built on the assumption that by developing awareness of their individual needs and values, underachieving students will be better able to establish meaningful goals and aspirations.

The intervention begins by having the student address the underachievement issue. Because the underachieving students involved in this program are by definition not meeting their academic potential (i.e., college GPA is significantly lower than ACT scores and high school grades would predict), the issue does not need to be established by the counselor. The student is asked to describe his or her high school academic experience and/or his or her college academic experience. The counselor can then begin to explore with the student the reasons for the differences in these experiences. In the event that major personal, academic, financial, or other problems arise, the counselor will make appropriate referrals.

The intervention then follows a test interpretation procedure used with honors students with particular emphasis placed on positive comments and withholding of value judgments. The intervention will conclude with a translation of values and needs into meaningful career and personal goals. A possible outcome of this intervention is that goal orientation will provide the motivation necessary for the student to improve academically. Another possible outcome is that the student will realize that his or her needs would best be filled outside the college environment.

## Intervention Script for Underachievers

I. Introduction

II. Have client explain underachieving history
  A. Ask about high school academic experience.
  B. Ask about college experience.
  C. Ask about the difference between each. Look for reasons for differences.

III. Fit intervention into history
  A. Describe purpose of interview.
    1. Better understanding of self.
    2. Relating of values to future goals.
    3. Benefit of defining future goals in terms of values.
  B. Describe purpose of tests.

IV. Discuss test results
  A. Vocational Personality Inventory
    1. Discuss code with hexagon.
    2. List Occupation Finder information.
    3. Look for unusual career combinations.
    NOTE: Make a comment about having a vocation, not just a career.
  B. Personality Research Form
    1. Discuss top three and bottom three needs.
    2. Look for consistencies and inconsistencies in needs.
  C. Rokeach Values Survey
    1. Ask if student wants to change ranking; discuss top scores.
    2. Relate values to each other. Support comments.
    3. Relate values and needs.

NOTE: Make a comment about achieving self-actualization through combining values and goals.

V. Summary
  A. Discuss need for making decisions based on values and needs.
  B. Summarize test results and how they fit together with questionnaire.
  C. Relate specific career possibilities to values; seek feedback.
  D. Address any other problems uncovered by history or during session; make appropriate referrals.

VI. Influence intervention
  Now that you've taken a close look at yourself—the values, needs and interests that make you who you are—you have a powerful tool to actualize your own full potential.

  Meaning is the key to finding direction. When you begin attuning your actions and decisions to your greatest values, you will find yourself more able to commit to goals—including some long-range plans—and to move toward them.

  Success in attaining these goals is directly related to the sense of purpose or mission that you feel underlies a particular course of action. If you take one thing away with you from this process, it should be the knowledge that you really can use your interests, values, and needs that we've discussed to mobilize your energies and create meaningful goals that maximize your potential.

VII. Conclusion
  Stress how much you have enjoyed working together. Point out that you're impressed by the client's willingness to learn about himself or herself and to apply this new knowledge to immediate and future decisions. Thank clients for sharing so much about themselves.

# Resources

Preliminary Scholastic Aptitude Test/
National Merit Scholarship Qualifying
Test/Scholastic Aptitude Test—administered by The College Board, The National Merit Scholarship Corporation,
and Educational Testing Service, respectively.

Addresses: The College Board
45 Columbus Ave.
New York, NY
10023–6917

The NMSC
One American Plaza
1560 Sherman Avenue
Evanston, IL 60201

ETS
1947 Center Street
Berkeley, CA
94704–2371
(also Princeton, NJ
08540)

ACT Assessment Program/P-ACT+

American College Testing
Program
2201 North Dodge Street
P.O. Box 168
Iowa City, IA 52243

# Major College Admissions and Advanced Placement Tests

Advanced Placement Examinations—administered by The College Board and Educational Testing Service

> The College Board
> 45 Columbus Ave.
> New York, NY 10023–6917

> Educational Testing Service
> (Berkeley Office)
> 1947 Center Street
> Berkeley, CA 94704–2371
> (also Princeton, NJ 08540)

# 5

## Resources

### Perfect Future Day Fantasy

Close your eyes . . . Relax your whole body . . . Relax completely . . . Imagine you are in a time machine, taking you into your own future. Imagine that it is 10 years from now. It's a weekday and you are waking. Is there someone there with you? . . . What time is it? . . . What's the season? . . . Climate? . . . Where are you? . . . Where do you live? . . . You're getting dressed now. What will you wear? . . . Where are you going today? . . . to work? . . . to school? Do you stay at home? . . . How will you get there? . . . What do you pass on the way? . . . Does it take long? . . . Now you've arrived . . . Where are you? . . . Are there buildings? What kind? . . . Do you go inside? . . . or perhaps you stay outside? . . . Are there people around? . . . Animals? . . . Plants? . . . Machines? . . . Books? . . . What is the first thing you do? . . . Next? . . . What will you do for the rest of the morning? . . . It's noon now and you are hungry. What will you do for lunch? . . . What kinds of food do you like? . . . How will you spend your afternoon? . . . Do you go back to the same place? . . . What's your favorite part of the afternoon? . . . How do you finish the afternoon? . . . Do you go home, or are you already there? . . . At home, what's it like? . . . What is your favorite room? . . . Is there anyone there? . . . What do you do after your day? . . . Soon, it's time for dinner . . . You eat. Has the sun set yet? . . . Is it early? . . . Now what will you do for the evening? It's getting late . . . What does the sky look like? . . . Are there any stars visible? . . . You go to bed . . . Now, bring yourself back to today . . . Imagine the room . . . Where are you? . . . Slowly open your eyes. . . .

## Goal Setting Sheet
## for Career Planning With Gifted Students

| GOALS | Goal 1: | Goal 2: |
|---|---|---|
| When do I want to reach this goal? | | |
| What can *I do* by tomorrow? | a.<br>b. | |
| By one week from now? | a.<br>b. | |
| Within 1 month? | a.<br>b. | |
| Further steps necessary? | a.<br>b. | |

# Biography
# Sources for
# Career
# Education*

Breen, Karen. *Index to Collective Biographies for Young Readers* (4th ed.). Bowker, 1988.
    Includes subject index of biographies, i.e., air pilots, archaeologists, etc.
*Outstanding Biographies for the College Bound*. American Library Association, 1987.
*Your Reading: A Booklist for Junior High and Middle School Students*. National Council of Teachers of English, 1988.

Biography Series

*American Women of Achievement Series*. Chelsea House.
*Black Americans of Achievement Series*. Chelsea House.
*Childhood of Famous Americans*. Aladdin.
*Dell Yearling Biography Series*. Dell.
*Great Lives Series*. (20th Century Politics and Government; Famous Explorers; Great Americans—each volume in each series is about

---

* Adapted from a bibliography prepared by Paula Brandt, Coordinator, Curriculum Resources Laboratory, College of Education, University of Iowa.

an individual—exs. Gorbachev, Kennedy, Tubman, Ride). Fawcett.

*Great Lives Series.* (Human Rights; American Government; Exploration; Sports—each volume is a collection of biographies). Scribner.

*My Life Series.* (As a Cartoonist; With the Chimpanzees; With the Dinosaurs; As an Astronaut) Dell.

*A Picture Book of. . .Series.* (Martin Luther King, Jr., Benjamin Franklin, Thomas Jefferson, George Washington, Abraham Lincoln, Helen Keller). Holiday House.

*Scholastic Biography Series.* Scholastic.

*Women of Our Time Series.* Viking (hardcover). Puffin (paperback).

*World Leaders, Past and Present Series.* Chelsea House.

# Resources

## Bibliography for Gifted Girls*

### Careers

Alexander, Sue. (1980). *Finding your first job.* Dutton.

Catalyst. (1980). *Marketing yourself: The Catalyst women's guide to successful resumes and interviews.* Putnam.

Catalyst. (1980). *What to do with the rest of your life: The Catalyst career guide for women in the 80's.* Simon.

Foote, Patricia. (1980). *Girls can be anything they want.* Messner.

Gilbert, Sara. (1979). *Ready, set go: How to find a career that's right for you.* Four Winds.

Gutman, Bill. (1982). *Women who work with animals.* Dodd.

Jochnowitz, Carol. (1978). *Careers in medicine for the new woman.* Watts.

Mitchell, Joyce Slayton. (1978). *I can be anything: Careers and colleges for young women.* College Entrance Examination Board.

Rogan, Helen. (1981). *Mixed company: Women in the modern Army.* Putnam.

---

* Adapted from "Career Planning for Young Women," bibliography prepared by Paula Brandt, Coordinator, Curriculum Resources Laboratory, College of Education, University of Iowa.

Rosenfeld, Megan. (1977). *Careers in journalism for the new woman.* Watts.
Skagen, Kiki. (1977). *Careers in education for the new woman.* Watts.
Skurzynski, Gloria. (1981). *Safeguarding the land: Women at work in parks, forests, and rangelands.* Harcourt.
Smith, Betsy Covington. (1981). *Breakthrough. Women in television.* Walker.
Smith, Elizabeth Simpson. (1981). *Breakthrough: Women in aviation.* Walker.
Wetherby, Terry. (Ed.). (1977). *Conversations: Working women talk about doing a "man's job."* Les Femmes.

# Biographies

Atkinson, Linda. (1985). *In kindling flame: The story or Hannah Senesh, 1921–1944.* Lothrop.
Bingham, Mindy. (1989). *Berta Benz and the motor wagon.* Advocacy.
Bober, Natalie S. (1984). *Breaking tradition: The story of Louise Nevelson.* Atheneum.
Brown, Marion Marsh. (1980). *Homeward the arrow's flight.* Abingdon.
Chadwick, Roxane. (1987). *Amelia Earhart: Aviation pioneer.* Lerner.
Chadwick, Roxane. (1987). *Anne Morrow Lindbergh: Pilot and poet.* Lerner.
Cleary, Beverly. (1988). *A girl from Yamhill: A memoir.* Morrow.
Deveaux, Alexis. (1980). *Don't explain: A song of Billie Holiday.* Harper.
Duden, Jane. (1988). *Shirley Muldowney.* Crestwood.
Evans, Mari. (Ed.). (1984, ©1983). *Black women writers (1950–1980): A critical evaluation.* Anchor/Doubleday.
Faber, Doris. (1985). *Margaret Thatcher, Britain's "Iron Lady."* Viking.
Ferris, Jeri. (1988). *Go free or die: A story about Harriet Tubman.* Carolrhoda.
Ferris, Jeri. (1988). *Walking the road to freedom: A story about sojourner truth.* Carolrhoda.
Fox, Mary Virginia. (1983). *Justice Sandra Day O'Connor.* Enslow.
Fox, Mary Virginia. (1984). *Women astronauts: Aboard the shuttle.* Messner.
Gherman, Beverly. (1986). *Georgia O'Keefe: The wideness and wonder of her world.* Atheneum.
Giff, Patricia Reilly. (1987). *Laura Ingalls Wilder: Growing up in the little house.* Viking.
Giff, Patricia Reilly. (1986). *Mother Teresa, Sister to the poor.* Viking.
Gilberg, Lynn, & Moore, Gaylen. (1981). *Particular passions: Talks with women who have shaped our times.* Potter.
Gish, Lillian. (1987). *An actor's life for me.* Viking.
Gleasner, Diana C. (1983). *Breakthrough: Women in science.* Walker.
Greene, Carol. (1984). *Louisa May Alcott: Author, nurse, suffragette.* Childrens.
Haskins, James. (1981). *Katherine Dunham.* Coward.

Haskins, James. (1983). *Lena Horne*. Coward.

Haskins, James. (1988). *Shirley Temple Black: Actress to ambassador*. Viking.

Henry, Dondra, & Taitz, Emily. (1987). *One woman's power: A biography of Gloria Steinem*. Dillon.

Jacobs, William Jay. (1983). *Eleanor Roosevelt: A life of happiness and tears*. Coward.

Keller, Mollie. (1983). *Golda Meir*. Watts.

Knudson, R. R. (1985). *Babe Didrickson, Athlete of the century*. Viking.

Knudson, R. R. (1986). *Martina Navratilova, Tennis power*. Viking.

Kudlinski, Kathleen V. (1988). *Rachel Carson: Pioneer of ecology*. Viking.

Laklan, Carli. (1980). *Golden girls: True stories of Olympic women stars*. McGraw.

Lawson, Don. (1985). *Geraldine Ferraro*. Messner.

McKissack, Patricia C. (1985). *Mary McLeod Bethune: A great American educator*. Childrens.

Meltzer, Milton. (1985). *Dorothea Lange: Life through the camera*. Viking.

Meltzer, Milton. (1986). *Winnie Mandel: The soul of South Africa*. Viking.

Meyer, Susan E. (1990). *Mary Cassatt*. Abrams.

O'Connor, Karen. (1984). *Literature*. Dillon.

Peavy, Linda, & Smith, Ursula. (1985). *Dreams into deeds: Nine women who dared*. Scribner.

Peavy, Linda, & Smith, Ursula. (1983). *Women who changed things*. Scribner.

Quackenbush, Robert. (1990). *Clear the cow pasture, I'm coming in for a landing*. Simon & Schuster.

Raven, Susan. (1981). *Women of achievement: Thirty-five centuries of history*. Harmony.

Reit, Seymour. (1988). *Behind rebel lines: The incredible story of Emma Edmonds, Civil War spy*. Harcourt.

Ride, Sally. (1986). *To space & back*. Lothrop.

Sabin, Francene. (1982). *Elizabeth Blackwell, The first woman doctor*. Troll.

Saunders, Susan. (1987). *Margaret Mead: The world was her family*. Viking.

Sheils, Barbara. (1985). *Winners: Women and the Nobel Prize*. Dillon.

Shor, Donnali. (1986). *Florence Nightingale*. Silver Burdett.

Siegel, Beatrice. (1988). *Cory: Corazon Aquino and the Philippines*. Dutton.

Sills, Leslie. (1989). *Inspirations: Stories about women artists*. Whitman.

Slatkin, Wendy. (1985). *Women artists in history: From antiquity to the 20th century*. Prentice.

Sullivan, George. (1985). *Mary Lou Retton: A biography*. Messner.

Tiburzi, Bonnie. (1984). *Takeoff! The story of America's first woman pilot for a major airline*. Crown.

Topalian, Elyse. (1984). *Margaret Sanger*. Watts.

Verheyden-Hilliard, Mary Ellen. (1985). *Scientist and governor, Dixy Lee Ray.* Equity.

Vinke, Hermann. (1984). *The short life of Sophie Scholl.* Harper.

Wenzel, Dorothy. (1990). *Ann Bancroft: On top of the world.* Dillon.

Wheeler, Leslie. (Ed.). (1981). *Loving warriors: Selected letters of Lucy Stone and Henry B. Blackwell, 1853 to 1893.* Dial.

Wilson, Dorothy Clarke. (1983). *I will be a doctor! The story of America's first woman physician.* Abingdon.

# Resources

## Books for Use in Counseling Gifted Students*

### Rationale and Suggested Uses

Most books for the gifted are recommended for their demanding intellectual content rather than for bibliotherapeutic purposes. The list that follows does contain demanding material but is intended primarily for the affective rather than the cognitive domain.

The idea of compiling such a list occurred to me several years ago when I was finishing my master's thesis on bibliotherapy and the gifted child. I became interested in discovering how many children's and adolescent novels were available that featured a gifted protagonist. The process of bibliotherapy—"helping with books"—is predicated on the reader's first identifying with a character in the book, which then allows for insight and catharsis to take place.

What better way to promote the crucial first step of identification than to

---

* By Stephen Schroeder-Davis, University of St. Thomas, St. Paul, Minnesota.

to have gifted readers meet gifted protagonists of similar ages, in similar settings, encountering similar problems, and experiencing similar joys and sorrows?

The titles listed below are the results of my research so far. Readers will be pleased to know that most of the fictional characters portrayed in these pages mirror quite well what research and experience tell us about gifted kids. Themes such as independence, multidimensionality, empathy, and concern for justice are found along with alienation, boredom in school, and perfectionism. It seems that the authors have either researched the field, have an accurate intuition, or more probably, are writing from experience. Furthermore, I found most of the books to be extremely well written and remarkably free of racism and sexism.

## How To Use This List

The books are listed alphabetically by author. Additional information includes the publisher, publication date, primary talent or gift in evidence (when such a distinction could be made) and a recommended interest/difficulty level. The last two items are very subjective. Because these fictional children are so much like their actual gifted counterparts, they often have several gifts, so the determination of "general intelligence" over "creativity" was somewhat arbitrary. More difficult still was a suggested target audience. Because many gifted children read beyond their assigned grade level by many years, these were necessarily subjective judgments. In general I assumed gifted children would be more interested in reading about gifted age peers, and so the recommendations often refer to the age of the protagonist in the hope that this will be more likely to encourage identification within the reader.

Parents and teachers are encouraged to examine the books and read them first if at all possible to help ensure a "match" between the suggested book and the reader.

The annotations are necessarily short but contain, whenever possible, a plot summary and major conflict area that seem to be the most critical story elements that users of this list need.

Appleton, Victor, II.
Tom Swift and His Diving Seacopter. Series..
New York: Grosset & Dunlop, 1956.
Special Talent: Math and Science. Elementary-Junior High.

Perhaps the seminal series honoring the intellect and inventiveness, these books all follow Tom Swift, the boy genius, as he solves the world's problems with his extraordinary mind and brilliant inventions. The language may sound dated, but the books are still fun to read and are great nostalgia.

Auel, Jean.
The Clan of the Cave Bear. Series.
New York: Crown, 1980.
General Intelligence. Creativity. Senior High.
Although set in prehistoric times, the analogy between Ayla, who is decidedly more advanced than her contemporaries, and gifted children and their age peers will be obvious and hopefully instructive to those who read this popular book.

Bottner, Barbara.
The World's Greatest Expert on Absolutely Everything Is Crying.
New York: Dell, 1986.
General Intelligence. Performing Arts. Upper Elementary.
A fine book that deals with perfectionism and the deleterious effects of unrealistic parental expectations. Katherine Ann, the new student in school, must balance her desire to be accepted among her peers with her parents' extraordinary demands and her own sometimes insensitive behavior.

Brooks, Bruce.
Midnight Hour Encores.
New York: Harper & Row, 1986.
Special Talent: Music. Junior-Senior High.
One of the few fictional titles that directly addresses the child prodigy, this is the story of Sibilance T. Spooner, world-class cellist. The enormous sacrifices and total devotion as well as the rewards and satisfaction of attaining world-class status are illustrated against the backdrop of a pair of mysteries about Sib's past and future.

Burningham, John. Illustrated by the author.
Time to Get Out of the Bath, Shirley.
New York: Crowell, 1978.
Special Talent: Creativity. Early Elementary.

Shirley loves to daydream in the bathtub. Sometimes she forgets the time and has to be reminded to get out! An excellent book for affirming introspection, daydreaming, and one's inner self for very young readers and their parents.

Cameron, Eleanor.
A Room Made of Windows. Series.
Boston: Little, Brown, 1971.
Special Talent: Writing. Junior-Senior High.
This novel abounds with characters gifted in both music and literature. Julia's friend Leslie has already been published (she's 13) and Julia, age 10, is submitting a manuscript. This is not an easy book, but well worth the effort, especially for aspiring writers.

Cole, Brock.
Celine.
New York: Farrar, Strauss, & Giroux, 1989.
Special Talent: Art. Junior-Senior High.
This book is not directly concerned with giftedness. Rather, we watch Celine, a 16-year-old, going through a rather difficult period in her life as she tries to deal with the various problems she encounters. Her love of art is evident throughout the book, but as background rather than the central focus. The author has won multiple awards.

Conford, Ellen.
And This Is Laura.
Boston: Little, Brown, 1977.
General Intelligence. Upper Elementary-Junior High.
Although virtually a straight-A student, Laura feels inadequate in a family of specialized superstars. Perhaps in compensation, she becomes psychic. Eventually, her gift becomes burdensome and she finally discusses her feelings of inadequacy with her parents, who are extremely affirming of her individuality, with or without her psychic abilities.

Cresswell, Helen.
Ordinary Jack. Series.
New York: Macmillan, 1977.
Multiple Talent Areas. Junior High.

As the title implies, the narrator in this story isn't "gifted"—but everyone else in his family is. This causes Uncle Parker to create a "gift" for Jack—clairvoyance! This is a tale told largely for humor and is part of a series about the Bagthorpes, all of whom have extreme talents and idiosyncrasies to match.

Dahl, Roald. Illustrated by Quentin Blake.
Matilda.
New York: Viking Penguin, 1988.
General Intelligence. Elementary.
Throughout the early chapters of this book, Dahl paints an incredibly touching portrait of an astonishingly gifted child virtually raising herself in a home that is decidedly anti-intellectual (the term "toxic parents" comes to mind). Later chapters become more fanciful, but no less amusing or effective.

Danziger, Paula.
The Cat Ate My Gymsuit. Sequel.
New York: Dell, 1974.
Special Talent: Verbal. Upper Elementary.
March Lewis has a poor self-image, largely because of her weight and unpopularity. She is very bright, however, and really begins to use her abilities when her English teacher is removed from class and March takes on the adult establishment in an attempt to have her reinstated.

Dixon, Franklin W.
The Shattered Helmet. Hardy Boys Series.
New York: Grosset & Dunlop, 1973.
General Intelligence. Upper Elementary.
Although perhaps not timeless literature, this series was among the first and most popular to portray intelligence and creativity as desirable traits useful in solving both everyday problems and life-threatening situations. An excellent bridge to more challenging literature. Despite the formulaic nature of these books, they provide good introductory role models.

Fitzgerald, John. Illustrated by Mercer Mayer.
The Great Brain. Series.
New York: Dell, 1967.
General Intelligence. Elementary.

Set in turn-of-the-century Utah, this series tells of Tom—the "Great Brain"—and the various nefarious schemes he hatches that utilize his intelligence—usually for profit. This is all in fun and makes for easy and enjoyable reading.

Fitzhugh, Louise.
Nobody's Family Is Going to Change.
New York; Farrar, Straus & Giroux, 1974.
General Intelligence. Special Talent: Dancing. Upper Elementary.
Another fine book by the author of *Harriet the Spy*, this is the story of would-be lawyer Emma and her brother Willie, an aspiring dancer. Because these are not stereotypical occupations, both kids encounter resistance and need lots of perseverance to pursue their dreams. A cautionary tale for parents who want their gifted children to be conventional.

Fitzhugh, Louise. Illustrated by the author.
Harriet the Spy.
New York: Harper & Row, 1964.
Special Talent: Verbal. Upper Elementary.
To exercise her writing abilities, Harriet keeps a candid diary containing covert observations on her neighbors and classmates. All is well until the diary is discovered. Harriet is then persuaded to use her abilities in more constructive and less injurious ways. An excellent look at a child who is determined to be an author.

Gardam, Jane.
Bilgewater.
New York: Willow Books, 1977.
General Intelligence. Junior High.
Although highly intelligent, Bilgewater is dyslexic. This problem masks her intelligence and adds to her feelings of isolation. She must battle both her handicap and her isolation to gain self-confidence. An excellent choice for children bearing the burden of a "double label."

Greene, Bette. Illustrated by Charles Lilly.
Philip Hall Likes Me. I Reckon Maybe. Sequel.
New York: Dell, 1974.
General Intelligence. Middle and Upper Elementary.

Beth and Philip are the two smartest kids in class, as well as rivals for most of the trophies and ribbons in school. If Beth has her way, they may someday become more than friends. But first Beth will have to learn to stop allowing Philip to win all the time, and Philip will have to learn he can't always be first.

Greene, Constance C. Illustrated by Byron Barton.
A Girl Called Al. Series.
New York: Viking, 1969.
General Intelligence. Upper Elementary.
Al is "a little on the fat side and a nonconformist." She is also very bright and not a little lonely. Through conversations reported by the book's unnamed narrator we watch Al deal with her weight, her isolation, and her entry into junior high. She receives help from Mr. Richards, the janitor in her building. This is the first book in the series.

Greenwald, Sheila.
Will the Real Gertrude Hollings Please Stand Up?
Boston: Little, Brown, 1983.
General Intelligence. Upper Elementary-Junior High.
Gertrude Hollings, considered learning disabled and an outcast at school but loved and cherished at home, must spend 3 weeks with her "perfect" and very competitive cousin Albert. To their mutual surprise, they find they can learn from one another. An excellent book to promote discussions about labels and stereotypes.

Gripe, Maria. Translated by Paul Britten Austin. Illustrated by Harald Gripe.
Hugo and Josephine.
New York: Delacorte, 1962.
Special Talent: Leadership. Psycho/Social. Early Elementary.
This is a story from Sweden about timid Josephine, who finds school easy but friendships difficult until the arrival of classmate Hugo. Hugo's quiet but fierce independence helps Josephine become accepted despite her shyness and love of books.

Hamilton, Virginia.
The Planet of Junior Brown.
New York: Dell, 1971.
Special Talent: Music. Junior High.

Junior Brown is prodigious in girth, ability, and degree of mental instability. His talents are not being realized and very few people are interested in or capable of understanding him. He does receive help, however, from two unlikely sources—a street-wise classmate and the school janitor.

Hodges, Margaret. Illustrated by W. T. Mars.
The Hatching of Joshua Cobb.
New York: Farrar, Straus & Giroux, 1967.
Special Talent: Leadership. Psycho/Social. Early Elementary.
Joshua's first summer camp is difficult until new counselor Dusty arrives. Josh looks up to him and would like to win a race in his honor. This proves impossible, as he finishes second each time. Dusty is able to help Josh resolve his disappointment, which should be instructive for young readers with a tendency toward perfectionism.

Hoover, H. M.
Treasures of the Morrow.
New York: Four Winds Press, 1976.
General Intelligence. Junior High.
This science fiction story, set in a post-holocaust society, tells of Tia and Rabbit, two gifted children who must escape their backward homeland where intelligence is reviled, to reach the land of Morrow, where intelligence is revered. The stark contrast between the two worlds may help gifted kids understand the ambivalence toward giftedness they may encounter.

Howe, James.
Eat Your Poison, Dear. Series.
New York: Atheneum, 1986.
General Intelligence. Upper Elementary-Junior High.
A "Sebastion Barth" mystery wherein Sebastion and his friends try to determine who is responsible for a series of lunchroom poisonings. Played entirely for fun, this series is in the mold of the Hardy Boys, but more contemporary.

Hughes, Dean. Illustrated by Blanche Sims.
Nutty for President. Series.
New York: Bantam, 1981.
General Intelligence. Upper Elementary.

Nutty Nutshell and his friends all attend the campus lab school and are all quite bright. No one, however, holds a candle to William Bilks, classmate and absolute genius. In William's role as advisor, he helps our hero realize most of his schemes. These stories are all in fun, but stress intelligence and problem solving.

Hunter, Mollie.
A Sound of Chariots.
New York: Harper & Row, 1972.
Special Talent: Verbal. Junior-Senior High.
The title, an allusion to the poem "To His Coy Mistress," embodies one of the themes—productive use of time—in this complex and beautiful novel. The self-actualization of narrator Bridie McShane is another major theme. She must overcome her father's death, adult insensitivity, and alienation from her peers before she can begin to realize her dreams.

Keene, Carolyn. Nancy Drew Series.
The Thirteenth Pearl.
New York: Grosset & Dunlop, 1979.
General Intelligence. Upper Elementary.
Another seminal series that exalts deductive abilities and intelligence as worthwhile attributes to possess. As with the Hardy Boys and Tom Swift, these books can function as a bridge to more difficult books as children's interests change and develop.

Key, Alexander.
The Forgotten Door.
Philadelphia: Westminster Press, 1965.
General Intelligence. Upper Elementary.
A boy with amazing powers and intelligence comes to earth by accident through a "forgotten door." His abilities are viewed with suspicion by virtually everyone, until a sympathetic family embraces him and helps him return to his home planet.

Keys, Daniel.
Flowers for Algernon. Entitled *Charlie* as a movie.
New York: Harcourt Brace Jovanovich, 1966.
General Intelligence. Secondary.

An open plea for tolerance of differences and the humane use of science, this seminal work tells the story of Charlie Gordon, a mildly retarded man who is given the "opportunity" to become exceedingly brilliant by virtue of an experimental operation. An extremely powerful book/movie combination.

Knowles, John.
A Separate Peace.
New York: Macmillan, 1960.
Special Talent: Leadership. Psychomotor. Junior-Senior High.
Although this novel was not intended specifically for the young adult market, all the major characters are teens, and the two major protagonists, Gene and Finny, are very bright. Finny is not just bright but has astonishing instincts and charisma, which causes much jealousy and leads ultimately to tragedy with a violent form of coercive egalitarianism.

Konigsburg, E. L. Illustrated by the author.
From the Mixed-Up Files of Mrs. Basil E. Frankweiler.
New York: Atheneum, 1967.
General Intellectual Ability. Upper Elementary.
Tired of being "straight A's Claudia Kincaid," Claudia persuades her brother to run away with her. They reside in New York's Metropolitan Museum of Art for a week where they solve a number of mysteries and learn about themselves in the process. Written by an award-winning author who consistently addresses issues of concern to gifted kids. This one was a Newbery winner.

Konigsburg, E. L. Illustrated by the author.
George.
New York: Dell, 1970.
General Intelligence. Identity. Upper Elementary.
Sixth grader Ben Carr is very bright and very imaginative. His imaginary friend George has been trying to warn him that his idol, a senior named William, is going to cause problems. Ben must learn to listen to and accept his "inner voice" if he is to stay true to himself.

Krumgold, Joseph. Illustrated by Alvin Smith.
Henry 3.
New York: Atheneum, 1967.
General Intelligence. Upper Elementary.

Henry views his 154 IQ as a handicap and actively hides his abilities until he develops a friendship with nonconforming Fletcher Larkin. Fletcher and a near disaster eventually convince Henry that it is dishonest to hide his talents, for they are an integral part of what he is.

L'Engle, Madeleine.
A Wrinkle in Time.
New York: Farrar, Straus, & Giroux, 1962.
General Intelligence. Creativity. Upper Elementary.
Ground-breaking and time-honored, this story, its
sequels, and much of L'Engle's other works offer protagonists who are both gifted and valued for their gifts within stories that are extremely well written and a joy to read. *A Wrinkle in Time* won the Newbery Award in 1963.

LeGuin, Ursula K.
Very Far Away From Anywhere Else.
New York: Atheneum, 1976.
General Intelligence. Music and Science. Junior High.
This is the story of two gifted teens, Owen Griffiths and Natalie Fields. It is Natalie, a gifted musician, who helps Owen embrace his intelligence and become more accepting of himself and his abilities. This is also a touching love story.

LeGuin, Ursula. Illustrated by James Brunsman.
Leese Webster.
New York: Atheneum, 1979.
Special Talent: Creativity. Preschool-Kindergarten.
A creative spider decides to spin beautiful variations from her traditional web. With assistance, students can see that being creative—or just being different—is something that should not merely be tolerated, but should be celebrated!

Leviten, Sonia.
The Mark of Conte.
New York: Macmillan, 1976.
General Intelligence. Junior-Senior High.
A mildly satiric look at high school life through the eyes of Conte Mark, who through computer error has received two class schedules

that he intends to follow simultaneously, thereby eliminating the necessity of a senior year. There are lots of bright kids in this book (in fact, they pretty much run the school) and they are all fun to read about.

Lowry, Lois.
Anastasia Krupnik.
Boston: Houghton Mifflin, 1979.
Special Talents: Verbal. Upper Elementary.
Anastasia loves to write and records her loves, hates, favorite words, and life's trials and tribulations in her notebook. An interesting and all-too-common conflict occurs between Anastasia and her teacher, who feels all poems must rhyme. Fortunately, her teacher later makes an effort to be kind, and Anastasia's parents are extremely supportive throughout.

MacLachlan, Patricia.
The Facts and Fictions of Minna Pratt.
New York: Harper & Row, 1988.
Special Talent: Music. General Intelligence. Upper Elementary.
Minna is surrounded by gifted and talented people: Her mother is an author, her father is a psychologist, her 10-year-old brother McGrew "knows everything" and she herself plays in a quartet of very talented musicians. She holds her own in this talented group as she practices her cello in search of the vibrato that "will allow her to play Mozart as he deserves to be played."

Mahy, Margaret.
The Tricksters.
New York: Scholastic, 1987.
Special Talent: Verbal. Junior-Senior High.
While on vacation, 17-year-old Harry and her family encounter three strangers. Harry, who is writing a novel, has insight into who and what the strangers are, and becomes involved with them despite the dangers they may bring. Author Mahy incorporates elements of the supernatural into this story.

Manes, Stephen.
Be a Perfect Person in Just Three Days!
New York: Bantam, 1982.
General Intelligence. Elementary.

A lighthearted look at the pitfalls of perfectionism, as Milo, with help from a clever professor in a book, finds that actually being perfect would be boring. A nonthreatening way to approach a difficult and problematic subject.

McDermott, Gerald. Illustrated by the author.
Anansi the Spider: A Tale From the Ashanti.
New York: Holt, Rinehart & Winston, 1972.
Multiple Talents. Preschool-Kindergarten.
This folklore tale tells of the rescue of Anansi from the inside of a fish, thanks to the heroics of his sons, each of whom is endowed with a unique talent. A good way to encourage children to embrace their individuality.

O'Brien, Robert C. Illustrated by Zena Bernstein.
Mrs. Frisby and the Rats of Nimh.
New York: Atheneum, 1971.
General (Enhanced) Intelligence. Upper Elementary.
The rats in the title are escapees from the National Institutes of Mental Health, where experiments have greatly enhanced their intellect. How they utilize their abilities to outwit and evade their would-be captors composes the majority of this adventure.

Oneal, Zibby.
In Summer Light.
New York: Bantam Books, 1981.
Special Talent: Art. Junior-Senior High.
An interesting look at giftedness through the eyes of talented but intimidated 17-year-old Kate Brewer. Her father is Marcus Brewer, world-famous artist and a very powerful figure. With help from Ian, who is serving as an intern with Marcus, Kate begins to forge an identity separate from her father, which eventually allows her to begin painting again.

Oneal, Zibby.
The Language of Goldfish.
New York: Viking, 1980.
Special Talent: Math. Art. Junior High.
A multifaceted look at giftedness from an author who consistently addresses such issues with insight and sensitivity. This novel tells

the story of Carrie Stokes's battles with anxiety and alienation that are severe enough to cause her to seek therapy. Her fight to overcome her problems could prove helpful to others with similar difficulties.

Paterson, Katherine.
Jacob I Have Loved.
New York: Crowell, 1980.
General Intelligence. Music. Junior High.
The second Newbery winner for Paterson, this is a story of sibling rivalry through the eyes of "older" twin Louise, who is jealous and resentful of her sister. It isn't until late in her teens that Louise is able to realize her own abilities and escape the long shadow cast by her twin.

Paterson, Katherine.
The Great Gilly Hopkins.
New York: Crowell, 1978.
General Intelligence. Upper Elementary.
This book deals with race, class, and adoption issues as seen through the eyes of embittered and abandoned young Gilly Hopkins. Gilly uses her intelligence to outwit adults, frustrate teachers, and torment children until, at long last, she meets loving, wise, accepting Maimie Trotter. Unfortunately, one of Gilly's past misdeeds will come back to haunt her.

Paterson, Katherine.
Come Sing, Jimmy Jo.
New York: Dutton, 1985.
Special Talent: Music. Upper Elementary.
James Johnson—"Jimmy Jo"—comes from a family of singers, but it isn't until a new agent encourages him to join his family on stage that his giftedness becomes a blessing and a curse. He must fight to express his giftedness and maintain his identity despite the difficulties inherent in being a celebrity.

Paterson, Katherine. Illustrated by Donna Diamond.
A Bridge to Terabithia.
New York: Crowell, 1977.
General Intelligence. Creativity. Visual Arts. Upper Elementary.

Jess feels isolated at home and at school. It isn't until Leslie comes and creates Terabithia that Jess begins to feel appreciated for who he really is. They become virtually inseparable. Then Jess has an opportunity to spend a day with Miss Edmunds, his favorite teacher, at an art gallery. While he is away tragedy strikes and Jess must learn to be strong alone.

Peck, Richard.
Remembering the Good Times.
New York: Delacorte, 1985.
General Intelligence. Junior High.
Narrator Buck Mendenhall, Kate Lucas, and gifted Trav Kirby have been friends since junior high and are about to start their sophomore year together. It is the second day of school when Buck and Kate are told that Trav has killed himself. They are left asking questions about death and suicide.

Peyton, K. M.
The Beethoven Medal.
New York: Crowell, 1971.
Special Talent: Music. Junior High.
A sequel to *Pennington's Last Term*, this story tells of the enormous dedication and frequent conflicts involved in the pursuit of a passion. Patrick Pennington must balance work and his love for the piano if he is to maintain his scholarship and become a concert performer.

Rand, Ayn.
Anthem.
New York: New American Library, 1946.
General Intelligence. Junior-Senior High.
Although Rand's theme, as always, is the individual against the collective, this early novel does a wonderful job of dealing with coercive egalitarianism in its most brutal and overt form. Virtually every gifted child will deal with this at some point, and it might be instructive to see the phenomenon in realistic terms.

Rodgers, Mary. Illustrated by the author.
Freaky Friday.
New York: Harper & Row, 1972.
General Intelligence. Upper Elementary.

One of the first books to employ the gimmick of switching bodies and minds—in this case Annabel Andrews with her mother—this book makes points about empathy, sensitivity, and using one's abilities, all in enjoyable fashion. Also a Disney movie.

Salinger, J. D.
The Catcher in the Rye.
Boston: Little, Brown, 1951.
General Intelligence. Junior-Senior High.
Perhaps the first "young adult" novel, this is the classic, often censored and always controversial story of Holden Caulfield, one of America's first alienated gifted kids. As sarcastic, vulgar, and profane as Holden can be, it is also obvious that he is bright, sensitive, and concerned with justice. The book is currently in its 69th printing.

Sebestyen, Ouida.
Words by Heart.
Boston: Little, Brown, 1968.
General Intelligence. Upper Elementary-Junior High.
Racial prejudice and small-minded envy make life difficult and ultimately tragic for Lena and her family. Lena's courage and willingness to express her abilities despite formidable obstacles are inspiring, as is her relationship with her heroic father. The ending is one of the most powerful displays of integrity and courage one can hope to find in a novel.

Sendak, Maurice. Illustrated by the author.
The Sign on Rosie's Door.
New York: Harper & Row, 1960.
Special Talent: Creativity. Preschool-Kindergarten.
Rosie is the neighborhood's most creative child, using her imagination to delight and entertain her friends during the long days of summer vacation.

Shreve, Susan. Illustrated by Diane deGroat.
The Flunking of Joshua T. Bates.
New York: Scholastic, 1984.
General Intelligence. Middle Elementary.

Despite his intelligence, Joshua flunks third grade. He learns this depressing fact on Labor Day, just before school resumes. Fortunately for Josh and his family, his new teacher, Mrs. Goodwin, sets out to correct the injustice done to Josh the previous year. With her help, Josh is able to pass the necessary tests and is promoted to fourth grade in less than 3 months.

Simon, Seymour. Illustrated by Fred Winkowski.
Einstein Anderson, Super Sleuth. Series.
New York: Viking, 1980.
General Intelligence. Science. Elementary.
This series features Einstein Anderson solving various puzzles and problems by applying scientific principles, logic, and his deductive abilities. In this book, he solves 10 mysteries by applying his knowledge of anatomy, technology, physics, acrobatics, zoology, meteorology, and biology!

Smith, Doris Buchanan.
Dreams and Drummers.
New York: Crowell, 1978.
Special Talents: Music, Verbal, and Science. Upper Elementary.
Perfectionism, multidimensionality, and the sometimes confusing gap between ability and maturation are all explored as 14-year-old Stephanie Stone tries to negotiate the often treacherous waters of junior high school. A direct look at some of the more important issues in the field by a talented author.

Sobol, Donald J. Illustrated by Leonard Shortall.
Encyclopedia Brown, Boy Detective. Series.
New York: Bantam, 1963.
General Intelligence. Elementary.
Leroy Brown, son of Idaville's police chief, is "Encyclopedia," so named because of his tremendous intellect and powers of reason. Most of these books come with 10 "cases," so readers can match wits with the amazing Leroy. Solutions are then given.

Thompson, Julian F.
Simon Pure.
New York: Scholastic, 1987.
General Intelligence. Junior-Senior High.

Radical acceleration is dealt with in this very light-hearted tale of Simon Storm, a 15-year-old college freshman. For Simon, classes are the least of his problems, what with woman trouble, his participation in a study of prodigies, and the possible takeover of the college by extremist republicans!

Tolan, Stephanie S.
  No Safe Harbors.
  New York: Fawcett Juniper, 1981.
  General Intelligence. Special Talents: Science. Moral Reasoning.
  Junior High.
    Coping skills and moral reasoning are emphasized in this novel. Narrator Amanda Sterling, her 10-year-old brother Doug, and new acquaintance Joe Schmidt all have difficulties due to aspects of their giftedness. Each solves problems in a unique way, which should be instructive to young readers.

Tolan, Stephanie.
  A Time to Fly Free.
  New York: Scribner, 1983.
  General Intelligence. Upper Elementary.
    Josh Taylor is both highly intelligent and almost unbearably sensitive. These two traits cause Josh to "drop out" of fifth grade—he simply walks away. With the insightful support of his stepfather, Josh is allowed to "do his own thing" while a more appropriate education is arranged. One of the things he does is discover a mentor who helps him realize his considerable gifts.

Voigt, Cynthia.
  Come a Stranger.
  New York: Ballantine Books, 1987.
  Special Talent: Dance. General Intelligence.
    Like all of Ms. Voigt's wonderful books, *Come a Stranger* is about many things. Mina is a very capable—but not a gifted—dancer. When she fails to be promoted with the rest of her class, she is not sure if she is a victim of prejudice or diminishing skill. Mina comes to terms with her heritage and her abilities in this fine story.

Williams, Jay, & Abrashkin, Raymond.
   Danny Dunn and the Homework Machine.
   New York: McGraw-Hill, 1958.
   Special Talent: Science. Elementary.
   A great book for students frustrated with "busy work," this is the
   story of Danny and his friends as they wrestle with the technical
   and ethical issues surrounding the invention of a "homework machine" that will eliminate the needless repetition of problems they
   already know the answers to.

# *Perfectionism Behavior Change Contract*

A. Waking up

1. Don't set your alarm. Wake up late. If your "body clock" wakes you up, go back to sleep or read a magazine until you are genuinely late.
2. Leave one item of grooming unfinished—hair unbrushed, shirt unpressed, or clothes unmatched.
3. Skip breakfast, or grab breakfast on the way to work or school.

B. At work/school

1. Let somebody down. Don't follow through on something that's not important to you.
2. Be late for a class or meeting you don't care much about; don't explain, don't apologize. During the time before the meeting, read something you're really interested in, or speak to someone you really care about.

C. Lunch

1. Don't count calories or read the menu carefully.
2. Eat what most appeals to you.
3. Take a longer time for lunch than you usually allow.

D. Afternoon

   1. Leave a task undone.
   2. Don't return an unimportant message.
   3. Leave as early as you can.

E. Dinner

   1. Eat whatever is there, without organizing or planning.

F. Evening assumes you'll do—wash dishes, take out the garbage.

   1. Let a family member down, or don't engage in some routine activity everybody assumes you'll do—wash dishes, take out the garbage.
   2. Don't finish your work.
   3. Go to bed late; read something you care about, or do something fun; or talk to a friend until late.

G. Next morning

   1. Start over.

# Role
# Stripping

The purpose of this exercise is to help you discover how your roles relate to your career goals and to help you better understand the roles that you assume. Hand out Role-Stripping sheet.

What are your most important roles?

Some examples are: student, friend, and so forth.

Write down the five most important roles you presently play. List them in order of their importance to you, 1 being the most important. Now tear off each of these roles so that you have five strips of paper, each with one role on it. Do you think they are in the right order? Put them in order, with the *least* important role on the top of your pile.

Now each of you will give up this least important role by going around the group and individually placing this strip of paper in the middle of the table, and talking to the rest of the group about how it feels not to have this role anymore. Any questions on this procedure?

I will give up my fifth role to get us started: (facilitator has her or his fifth role ready, and demonstrates).

(All participants give up fifth role).

Now we will give up our fourth role . . . third role . . . second role . . . . Now we will give up our last and probably most important role. This may be difficult to do.

(All participants have now given up all five roles.)

Now you have given up all five roles. How does that feel?

Close your eyes for a moment and imagine yourself without these roles. What do you feel? Who are you? You may open your eyes.

In a way, we *are* our roles. It is the responsibilities that go with each of these roles that give meaning to our lives.

Now you may take back the roles you want. Are there any you really don't want back? You may leave them on the table if you like. Perhaps you can think of other roles you might rather have.

Now how does it feel to have your roles back? (Elicit responses from group; not everyone need respond).

This can be a powerful exercise. Perhaps its impact will help you when you make decisions about a career. Some of your important roles may come into conflict with a particular career you're considering; or perhaps they will reinforce the decision for you.

(If anyone seems upset by this exercise, provide empathic response; ask for support from the group.)

*Additional
Resources*

## NATIONAL CENTERS FOR COUNSELING AND GUIDANCE OF THE GIFTED AND TALENTED

The Counseling Laboratory for Talent Development
Connie Belin National Center for Gifted Education
210 Lindquist Center
The University of Iowa
Iowa City, IA 52242

Gifted Child Development Center
P.O. Box 3489
Littleton, CO 80161
(303)798–0986

Guidance Laboratory for Gifted and Talented
131 Bancroft Hall
University of Nebraska-Lincoln
Lincoln, NE 68510

The Laboratory for Gifted at the Counselor Training Center
401 Payne Hall
Arizona State University
Tempe, AZ 85287

Supporting Emotional Needs of the Gifted
Wright State University
P.O. Box 2745
Dayton, OH 45401
(513)873–4306

# Talent Search
# Programs

ACT/SAT  Talent Identification
Program
Box 40077
Duke University
Durham, NC 27706
(919)684–3847
(919)683–1400
(Director's Office)

*16 states*

| | |
|---|---|
| Alabama | Mississippi |
| Arkansas | Missouri |
| Florida | Nebraska |
| Georgia | N. Carolina |
| Iowa | Oklahoma |
| Kansas | S. Carolina |
| Kentucky | Tennessee |
| Louisiana | Texas |

ACT/SAT  Midwest Talent Search
(MTS)
2003 Sheridan Rd.
Northwestern University
Evanston, IL 60208
(708)491–3782
Director—Dr. Paula
Olszewski-Kubilius

*8 states*

| | |
|---|---|
| Wisconsin | Minnesota |
| Illinois | S. Dakota |
| Indiana | N. Dakota |
| Michigan | Ohio |

ACT/SAT  Rocky Mountain Talent
Search
2135 E. Wesley Ave.
203 Wesley Hall
University of Denver
Denver, CO 80208
(303)671–2533
Director—Dr. Jill Burruss

*7 states*

| | |
|---|---|
| Colorado | New Mexico |
| Idaho | Utah |
| Montana | Wyoming |
| Nevada | |

Center for Talented Youth
3400 N. Charles St.
Johns Hopkins University
Baltimore, MD 21218
(301)338–8427
Director—Dr. William
   Durden

*20 states*

| | |
|---|---|
| Alaska | New Jersey |
| Arizona | New York |
| California | Oregon |
| Connecticut | Pennsylvania |
| Delaware | Rhode Island |
| Hawaii | Virginia |
| Maine | Vermont |
| Maryland | Washington |
| Massachusetts | W. Virginia |
| New Hampshire | District of Columbia |

# National
# Associations

American Association for Gifted Children
c/o Wright State University
P.O. Box 2745
Dayton, OH 45401
(513)873–4300

National Association for Gifted Children (NAGC)
1155 15th St. NW, #1002
Washington, DC 20005
(202)785–4268

National/State Leadership Training Institute for Gifted and Talented
   (NSLTI/GT)
Hilton Center
900 Wilshire Boulevard; Suite 1142
Los Angeles, CA 90017
(213)489–7470

Gifted Child Society, Inc.
190 Rock Road
Glen Rock, NJ 07452
(201)444–6530

The Council for Exceptional Children (CEC) and the Association for
   the Gifted (TAG)
1920 Association Drive
Reston, VA 22091
(703)620–3660

The ERIC Clearinghouse on Handicapped and Gifted Children
1920 Association Drive
Reston, VA 22091
(703)620–3660

The World Council for the Gifted and Talented
Box 218
Teachers College
Columbia University
New York, NY 10027
(212)678–3877

# *Periodicals*

*Gifted Child Quarterly*
National Association for Gifted Children (NAGC)
1155 15th St. NW, #1002
Washington, DC 20005
(202)785–4268

*Journal for the Education of the Gifted* (JEG)
The Association for the Gifted
1920 Association Drive
Reston, VA 22091
(703)620–3660

*Journal of Counseling & Development*
American Association for Counseling and Development
5999 Stevenson Avenue
Alexandria, VA 22304–3303
(703)823–9800

*Roeper Review*
P.O. Box 329
Bloomfield Hills, MI 48073
(313)642–1500 (Subscription) (313)971–3302 (Larry Gessen, Editor)

*Understanding Our Gifted*
Snowpeak Publishing, Inc.
P.O. Box 3489
Littleton, CO 80161
(303)798–0986

*Educational Opportunity Guide: A Directory of Programs for the Gifted*
Talent Identification Program
01 West Duke Building
Duke University
Durham, NC 27708
(919)684–3847

*The Gifted Child Today*
P.O. Box 637
100 Pine Avenue
Holmes, PA 19043